Spanish
False Friends
and Other Traps

Raúl Gáler

Spanish
False Friends
and Other Traps

A Guide to Translating
English Into/From Spanish

Hippocrene Books, Inc.
New York

Copyright © 2008 Raúl Gáler

For information, address:
   Hippocrene Books, Inc.
   171 Madison Ave.
   New York, NY 10016
   www.hippocrenebooks.com

Library of Congress Cataloging-in-Publication Data

   Gáler, Raúl.
      Spanish false friends and other traps : a guide to translating English into/from Spanish / Raúl Gáler.
         p. cm.
   Includes index.
   ISBN 978-0-7818-1178-1 (alk. paper)
      1. Spanish language—Translating into English. 2. English language—Translating into Spanish. I. Title.

   PC4498.G35 2008
   468'.0221—dc22   2007031765

Printed in the United States of America.

Contents

*To the women in my life—
my wife and three daughters.*

Foreword – *Prefacio*

My interest in languages, prior to my professional activity, dates from childhood. At one point in his life, my father worked as a merchant sailor, settled in San Francisco and became an American citizen. He subsequently returned to Argentina and got married. I inherited his taste for travel and languages. As a child, I was an avid reader of cheap Spanish editions of world literature, and soon realized that I could not understand some books properly unless I had read the originals. Those were my first encounters with false friends. I was to become better acquainted with them in my professional life.

This book tries to capture some of my experience with these expressions, in particular at the United Nations. Although not a trained theoretical linguist, I knew that words have the strangest way of evolving from their origins, taking diverging paths to a wide variety of destinations. Living in New York I witnessed the progress of "Spanglish." The influence of English was strong enough to

Mi interés por los idiomas, antes que el uso profesional que he hecho de ellos, data de mi infancia. Mi padre, que en algún momento de su vida era marino mercante, ancló en San Francisco y llegó a ser ciudadano de Estados Unidos. Luego, volvió a la Argentina y se casó. Heredé su gusto por los viajes y las lenguas. De niño, leía ávidamente ediciones baratas de la literatura universal, para comprobar que muchas veces necesitaba haber conocido los originales para comprenderlas bien. Fue mi primer encuentro con los falsos amigos. Llegué a tratarlos más en mi vida profesional.

Este libro trata de reflejar algo de mi experiencia de ellos, recogida muy especialmente en las Naciones Unidas. Aunque no soy lingüista de formación, supe que las palabras tienen la rara cualidad de evolucionar desde sus orígenes por caminos distintos hacia destinos diferentes. Y por vivir en Nueva York, fui testigo del avance del spanglish. Pero la influencia del inglés ha sido, sí, sustancial

penetrate a very rich language, with or without justification. Here, I also try to deal with cases of copycat words or different intrusions into Spanish.

I realize, of course, that there would be no Romance languages today if the Roman legions had not swept through Europe. However, I question the need for borrowing already existing words or expressions from foreign languages for which equivalents already exist in the native language. This is obviously not the case for many notions in science and technology that have served to enrich our vocabulary. English and Spanish are spoken by millions of people in many countries, by more speakers than most other languages, including French, Arabic, Chinese, or Swahili. In any case, the cultural impact here is unparalleled.

* * *

When examining words that could mislead a translator, I have paired not only words of the same etymology, but also those in which the spelling is almost the same. I have taken the liberty of also listing some odd expressions that might confuse the interpreter or a person who has not completely mastered the language, particularly colloquial American and Latin

al penetrar un idioma ya rico, con o sin justificación. Aquí, he de tratar también de examinar los calcos o las distintas invasiones en español.

Comprendo que hoy no habría lenguas romances si las legiones romanas no hubieran viajado por el resto de Europa, pero impugno la necesidad de tomar palabras o expresiones para nociones que ya estaban presentes y que no añadían nada. No es el caso, por supuesto, de muchos conceptos científicos o tecnológicos y hasta de la vida cotidiana que han enriquecido nuestro vocabulario. El inglés y el español son hablados por millones de personas en muchos países, más que la mayoría de los demás idiomas, incluso el francés, el árabe, el chino o el swahili. En todo caso, su influencia cultural no tiene comparación.

* * *

Al estudiar las palabras que pudieran confundir a un traductor, decidí comparar no solo las voces de igual etimología sino también otras que se escriban lo mismo o casi igual. Me he tomado también la libertad de enunciar algunas expresiones curiosas que pudieran desconcertar al intérprete o a quien no domine del todo la lengua en su uso en los Estados Unidos o en

American usage. The Glossary, however, is not a substitute for a dictionary, and will not list words that have the same meaning in both languages, except as a means for illustrating their most common meanings. The entries (in Spanish) are arranged alphabetically.

algunos países latinoamericanos. Pero el Glosario no pretende reemplazar a un diccionario, y no incluye palabras con igual significado en ambos idiomas, como no sea como medio de ilustrar los sentidos más comunes. El glosario sigue el orden alfabético en español.

Acknowledgments – *Agradecimientos*

I wish to thank my editors, especially Monica Bentley, who carefully edited the original copy, and to those who from the very beginning of this project gave me the benefit of their expertise and advice: Lynn Visson, Jesús Baigorri, Bruce Boeglin, Carol Martínez, and Stephen Pearl. They were kind enough to fill in the gaps of my academic shortcomings, though they could not always overcome my stubborn insistence on various points. And I must reiterate the platitudinous phrase that I alone, of course, take the responsibility for any errors.

Vaya mi reconocimiento a mis editores, especialmente a Monica Bentley, que hizo una revisión cuidadosa del original, y a quienes me prestaron desde el comienzo sus conocimientos y consejos: Lynn Visson, Jesús Baigorri, Bruce Boeglin, Carol Martínez, y Stephen Pearl. Amablemente suplieron mis carencias académicas, no siempre mi empecinamiento en insistir en algunas cosas. Aunque suene repetido, los errores son totalmente míos, por supuesto.

Spanish – English Glossary

ABATIMIENTO. *Abatimiento* is synonymous with *depression, dejection.* (**El final del romance le causó gran abatimiento.** The end of the affair left him very depressed.)

ABATEMENT. *Abatement* indica la *tasa de una reducción.* (**There is an abatement of the property tax for apartments up to a certain value.** El impuesto inmobiliario se rebaja para los departamentos de cierto valor.)

ABATIR. *Abatir* means *to knock down, to demolish, cut down.* (**La policía abatió al delincuente en el tiroteo.** The police gunned down the criminal.)

ABATE. *To abate* significa *rebajar, reducir* una cuenta, impuesto o interés; *amenguar* o *remitir.* (**The new legislation proposed to abate property taxes for a household's sole residential property.** En la nueva ley se propone reducir el impuesto inmobiliario en el caso de única propiedad de residencia familiar. **The storm abated.** Amenguó la tormenta.)

ABOGACÍA. *Abogacía* is the profession of lawyers, solicitors, etc. (**Eligió la carrera de abogacía.** He chose law as a profession.)

ADVOCACY. Se designa con *advocacy* la *promoción o defensa* de una causa. (**Many nongovernmental organizations undertake the advocacy of human rights.** Muchas organizaciones no gubernamentales se ocupan de la defensa de los derechos humanos.)

ABREVIATURAS, SIGLAS. A translator has to face the problems posed by acronyms or abbreviations that are not clarified with subsequent text, as used to be the usual editorial practice. Although this is prevalent in English, it has also become common in Spanish. Sometimes abbreviations cross language lines, with the reader left wondering what they mean. *PC* (originally *Partido Comunista* in Spanish) may also mean *Personal Computer* or *Politically Correct*/***Políticamente Correcto***.

ABBREVIATIONS, ACRONYMS. Se solía aclarar una sigla la primera vez que se presentaba en un texto, pero hoy se presume que el lector u oyente ya la conoce, cosa que perturba bastante en las conferencias, por ejemplo. Algunas se mantienen en el original inglés, aunque hoy muchas se han adaptado al español. Las hay que se mantienen por mayor eufonía, como **UNESCO** (Organización de las Naciones Unidas para la Educación, la Ciencia y la Cultura), otras que se han incorporado al lenguaje, como **radar** (*radio detecting and ranging*, *detección y localización por radio*). **Posh** (término marino que significa **port out, starboard home**, camarote de babor de salida, de estribor de regreso, por *cómodo, elegante*), **laser** (*light amplification by stimulated emission of radiation*, *amplificación de luz mediante emisión inducida de radiación*), **snafu** (*situation normal, all fouled up*, *situación normal, todo enredado* [jerga militar]); pero otros, como **WMD** (*weapons of mass destruction*); **24/7** (abierto las 24 horas, todos los días); **9 to 5** (empleo burocrático, de 9 de la mañana a 5 de la tarde) pueden ser un misterio para los no iniciados.

Abstracto. In Spanish, this word only means the opposite of concrete. (**Piensa en abstracto, sin concretar sus ideas.** He thinks in the abstract, without expressing concrete ideas.)

Abstract. Aparte del sentido contrario a concreto, con esta voz se designa el *resumen ejecutivo* o *resumen*, una *versión abreviada* de un ensayo, una tesis universitaria o una comunicación científica a una institución universitaria. (**Before each contribution to the congress, an abstract in the Proceedings gives you the main lines.** Antes de cada colaboración para el congreso, hay en los Anales un resumen ejecutivo que contiene sus principales ideas.)

Abusar. *Abusar* in Spanish means an *exaggerated use* of something. (**Abusa de los calificativos.** He makes too much use of adjectives.)

Abuse. La voz inglesa tiene una gama más amplia de equivalencias en español, que van de *abusar* a *maltratar*, *injuriar*, *insultar*. (**Liberals were the object of abuse at the demonstration.** En la manifestación se insultó a los liberales.)

Abusivo. *Abusivo* means an exaggerated or inappropriate use of something. (**Es abusiva la publicidad en la television.** There is far too much advertising on TV.)

Abusive. En ingles, la palabra significa *injurioso*, *ofensivo*, *insultante*. (**His language is abusive.** Se expresa de manera insultante.)

ACADEMIA. Spanish has kept closer to the original meaning of this word, which is defined by the Dictionary of the Royal Spanish Academy as a *scientific or literary institution*, generally publicly funded. (**En todos los países hispanohablantes hay academias de la lengua correspondientes de la Real Academia Española.** All Spanish-speaking countries have language academies that correspond to the Spanish Royal Academy.)

ACADEMIA. La voz inglesa va más allá de la española, para aplicarla al *ambiente universitario, erudito y de investigación*. (**He had a strong background in academia.** Tenía un curriculum muy sólido en la actividad universitaria.)

ACCEDER. *Acceder* is *to give one's consent, agree, accept.* (**El patrón accedió a la solicitud de aumento.** The boss agreed to the request for a raise.)

ACCEDE, ACCESS. *To accede*, en cambio, es *tener acceso* a un lugar o *adherir a un convenio internacional*. (**Nowadays, most handicapped persons have access to buses.** Hoy, muchos minusválidos tienen acceso a los autobuses. **Many countries acceded to the convention on the suppression of terrorism.** Muchos países adhirieron al convenio sobre represión del terrorismo.)

ACCESORIO. *Accesorio* is a *part* of a vehicle or machine. It is derived from the principal meaning of secondary. (**Este dispositivo es accesorio.** This is a secondary device.)

ACCESSORY. Un importante sentido de *accessory* es el de *cómplice*. (**The driver of the escape car was convicted as an accessory to the robbery.** El conductor del automóvil utilizado para huir fue condenado como cómplice del robo.)

ACCIDENTE. In addition to the normal meaning of this pair, *accidente* can mean a *feature*, as in *accidente geográfico*. (**Bahía, estrecho, península son accidentes geográficos.** Bay, strait, peninsula are geographical features.)

ACCIDENT. Aparte de la acepción de *accidente*, vale la pena notar que también se usa la palabra *incident* para referirse a accidente de poca monta. También está *near miss*, básicamente en aviación para lo que casi llegó a accidente. (**Reduced separation between airliners nearly caused an accident.** Por la poca separación entre aeronaves casi se produjo un accidente.)

ACCIÓN. Sometimes, *acción* may be translated as *action* or *deeds*. (**A la palabra debe seguir la acción.** Words must be followed by action.) *Acción* has another meaning, that of *stock* or *share*. (**Las acciones de Pfizer subieron un 10%.** Pfizer shares appreciated 10%.)

ACTION, AUCTION. *To take action* es *tomar una decisión*, adoptar una medida final. (**The meeting proceeded to take action on the proposal.** La sesión pasó a decidir sobre la propuesta.) Pero muy distinto es *auction*, *subasta*. En tanto que acción deriva del Latín *agere, hacer, auction* viene del Latín *augere, aumentar*. (**The auction confirmed the value of his paintings**. La subasta confirmó el valor de sus cuadros.)

ACOMODAR. The Spanish word *acomodar* may be translated as *to arrange* or, as applied to an usher (*acomodador*), *to seat* someone in a theater or concert hall. (**Acomodó los papeles sobre el escritorio.** He organized the papers on the desk.) *Una persona acomodada* is someone who is well off.

ACCOMMODATE. *To accommodate* significa *avenirse* a algo o alguien. (**The husband accommodated his wife's wishes.** El marido se avino a complacer a la esposa.)

ACTITUD. In Spanish this word is neutral. (**Su actitud es correcta.** He has the right attitude.)

ATTITUDE. En inglés a veces el sentido de *attitude* (y de sus derivados *attitudinal, attitudinize*) se limita a una *actitud afectada, exagerada o de pocos amigos*. (**Of the whole audience, it was he who showed an attitude.** De todo el público, fue él quien mostró una actitud desagradable.) *Véase opinionated.*

ACTIVO. Two words with exactly the same meaning, except for one use in Spanish: *activo* is the part of the balance sheet that lists the *assets*, contrary to *pasivo*, the *liabilities*. (**El activo reflejaba la riqueza de la sociedad.** The company's assets were a proof of its solidity.)

ACTIVE. *Active* quiere decir *activo* en la acepción de algo o alguien que no está en descanso, pero nunca en la acepción contable, de *assets*.

ACTUAL, ACTUALIDAD. *Actual* is what happens *today, at present*, and the same idea is conveyed by *actualidad*. (**Mis intereses actuales son distintos de los de mi juventud.** My present day interests are different from those of my youth. **La actualidad política es desalentadora.** Today's politics are disappointing.)

ACTUAL, ACTUALITY. *Actual* es la *realidad*, lo que pasa en verdad, los hechos. (**The actual value of the company has been reduced by the merger.** El valor real de la empresa ha disminuido debido a la fusión. **In actuality, he lost money with the investment.** En realidad, perdió dinero en la inversión.)

ADECUADO. (**Viste más que de manera adecuada para la fiesta.** His attire is more than adequate for the party.)

ADEQUATE. A veces *suficiente* es mejor traducción para *adequate*. (**They lacked adequate funding for their project.** Les faltó dinero suficiente para su proyecto.)

ADJUDICAR. In Spanish this word has a wider range: to *assign*, *allocate* or *appropriate*. (**Se adjudica esa cita a Churchill.** That quotation is attributed to Churchill.)

ADJUDICATE. *Adjudicate* se usa en sentido estrictamente jurídico: *decidir en favor* de una de las partes en un juicio. (**The judge adjudicated in favor of the plaintiff.** El juez falló en favor del demandante.)

ADVERTENCIA. *Advertencia* is a *warning*. (**El Departamento de Estado hizo una advertencia a posibles turistas a esa región.** The State Department issued an advisory to prospective tourists to that region.)

ADVERTISEMENT. *Advertisement* es un *anuncio publicitario*, que en América Hispana también se designa como *aviso*. (**Cigarette advertisement is restricted in public places.** Se limita la publicidad de cigarrillos en lugares públicos.)

AGENDA. A *notebook* for addresses and daily reference is *una agenda*. With the progress of technology, there are now *agendas electrónicas* to keep all those data in a pocket-size machine. (**Olvidé mi agenda con todas las direcciones.** I left behind my diary with all the addresses.) *Agenda* is beginning to also be used in the English sense. (**El ministro tiene una agenda muy cargada.** The minister has a heavy agenda.)

AGENDA. En la terminología de conferencias, the *agenda* es el *orden del día*. (**There were controversial items on the agenda of the meeting.** Había temas polémicos en el orden del día de la reunión.) *Hidden agenda* quiere decir un *propósito oculto* o *accesorio*. (**His apparently innocuous proposal covered a hidden agenda.** Su propuesta aparentemente inocua encubría un propósito oculto.)

AGONÍA. In a figurative sense, *agonía* is a synonym of *maximum anxiety* or *pain*. (**La agonía de la espera le resultaba insoportable.** He could not stand the agony of waiting. **Ya en la agonía, recibió la extremaunción.** About to die, he received extreme unction.)

AGONY. Se trata aquí de señalar la mayor frecuencia con que se emplea el sentido figurado, similar en ambos idiomas. (**He lived in agony waiting for news of the accident.** Vivía aterrorizado esperando noticias del accidente.)

AGONIZAR. In Spanish it means to *be about to die*, but also to *suffer enormously*.

AGONIZE. *Atormentarse, desesperarse.* (**The student agonized waiting for his grades.** El estudiante, afligido, esperaba sus notas.)

AGRADABLE. The Spanish adjective derives from the verb *agradar* (*to please*). (**Tiene un carácter muy agradable.** He has the nicest disposition.)

AGREEABLE. *Agreeable* viene de *to agree* (*aceptar, convenir*), que nada tiene que ver con agradable (que se traduce por *nice, pleasant*). (**His latest offer was considered agreeable.** Su oferta más reciente se consideró aceptable.)

AGRAVACIÓN. *Agravación* expresses exclusively the *worsening of a condition*, a *turn for the worse*, and not the English usage. (**La agravación de su mal fue sorpresiva, después de su mejora del día anterior.** His condition worsened unexpectedly, following his improvement on the previous day.)

AGGRAVATION. Casi siempre quiere decir *irritación*. (**Not only was he not on time, but she had the aggravation of having to wait in the cold.** No sólo fue él impuntual, sino que ella debió pasar frío esperándolo.)

AGRAVAR. The basic meaning of the word is expressed by *to take a turn for the worse*. (**La enfermedad se agravó inesperadamente.** Unfortunately, the disease took a turn for the worse.)

AGGRAVATE. Con gran frecuencia esta palabra se escucha en la conversación con el sentido de *irritar*, *molestar*.

AGRESIVO. This word has in Spanish the usual meaning of *menacing*, *violent*, and no other. (**Tenía un tono de voz agresivo.** The tone of his voice was aggressive.)

AGGRESSIVE. En inglés, aparte de la significación original, esta palabra denota *firmeza*, *determinación o ambición*, que no tiene por qué ser violenta. (**She aggressively pursued her research.** Llevó la investigación de modo decidido.) ***Aggressive executives*** puede traducirse como *ejecutivos emprendedores*.

AGRÍCOLA. *Agrícola* is what refers to *agriculture*, but also to the *agro*, the countryside in general. For instance, there is no equivalent in English for the term *agrícolaganadero* (or *agropecuario*, for that matter), used in certain countries, *ganadería* (cattle raising, livestock) being part of the *agro* business. (**La Argentina es un país de gran riqueza agrícolaganadera.** Argentina is a country of great agricultural wealth.)

AGRICULTURAL. *Agricultural* es el equivalente exacto of *agrícola*, con la salvedad anotada en la columna de la izquierda, de que comprende la ganadería. (**Fifty percent of the population is engaged in agricultural activity.** El 50% de la población se dedica a la actividad agrícola.)

ALOCAR. *Alocar* is *to render insane*. (**El chocolate lo aloca.** He is crazy about chocolate.)

ALLOCATE. *To allocate* es *asignar*, nada que ver con loco, para lo que se emplearía *mad*, *insane*, *crazy*. (**Not enough money was allocated to this item of expenditure.** No se asignó suficiente dinero a esta partida presupuestaria.)

ALTERAR. The word has a similar meaning to *alter*: *to modify*, *to change*. However, *alterar* is also used in the sense of *to distress*, *to disturb*. (**Le alteró la noticia.** The news distressed him.)

ALTER. *To alter* se usa en la acepción de *arreglar* (*ropa*). De ahí, *alteration*. (**After the alteration, the suit was a perfect fit.** El traje, una vez arreglado, le sentó de maravilla.)

ALTERNAR. Same meaning as *alternate*.

ALTERNATE. Es mejor en la mayoría de los casos traducir **to alternate** por *turnarse*. (**By agreement between the two political parties, they alternated in the presidency.** Por acuerdo entre los dos partidos politicos, se turnaban en la presidencia.)

ALTERNATIVA. Even if the English meaning (a proposition different from the initial one) is now widely used in Spanish, strictly speaking *alternativa* is a proposition that has two options. (**La alternativa es ir a la playa o a la montaña en verano.** In summer, the choice is the beach or the mountain.)

ALTERNATIVE. En la frase **The opposition proposed an alternative to the motion**, se ve que *alternative* quiere decir *algo diferente*. (**Let's take a walk or, as an alternative, go to the gym.** Caminemos, o si no, vayamos al gimnasio.)

ALUMNO, ALUMNA. *Alumno* or *alumna* is someone who takes courses at a school or college. (**El sabio profesor prepara a sus alumnos.** The scholar prepares his students.)

ALUMNA, ALUMNUS. Las voces inglesas, derivadas del latín, designan a los *ex alumnos* con respecto a su universidad. (**He is a Yale alumnus.** Es un antiguo alumno de Yale.)

AMENIDAD. This word gives the idea of *pleasantness, friendliness.* (**La amenidad de la reunion compensó la fala de comida.** The meeting was so entertaining that it made up for the lack of food.)

AMENITY. En ingles, además del sentido señalado en la columna de la izquierda, *amenities* denota las comodidades o cualidades de una vivienda. (**The apartment had all the modern amenities.** El apartamento tenía todas las comodidades modernas.)

AMÉRICA. *América* refers to all of the Americas, from Canada and Alaska to Tierra del Fuego. *Americano* is the usual adjective of nationality for *American,* with a minority using *estado-unidense. Iberoamericano, Latinoamericano,* and *Sudamericano* have thus become the words applied to non-US. Some even call *sudamericano* those hailing from Mexico or the Caribbean. The music known as *Latina* is mainly Caribbean.

AMERICA. El nombre oficial *United States of America* suele abreviarse en los Estados Unidos especialmente como *America*, y se conoce a sus ciudadanos como *American.*

ANGINA. In both languages, *angina* is the serious health condition known as *angina pectoris.* (**La angina lo ha confinado en la cama.** He has to stay in bed because of his angina.)

ANGINA. En sentido estricto, aunque *angina* quiere decir *angina pectoris*, se usa raramente como sinónimo de *amigdalitis* o *tonsilitis.*

Ansioso. To be *ansioso* is *to have a strong desire, to be impatient about something.* (**Está ansioso por conocer los resultados del análisis.** He anxiously awaits the test results.)

Anxious. En lugar de *ansia vehemente*, como en el ejemplo de la izquierda, el término inglés denota no sólo impaciencia, sino también temor y preocupación. (**He anxiously awaits the result of the operation.** Espera preocupado el resultado de la operación.)

Antigüedad, Antiguo. *Antigüedad* is a word that does not raise any problem. (**Las antigüedades mayas tienen precios prohibitivos.** Maya antiques have unaffordable prices. **Es una costumbre que nos viene de la antigüedad.** This is a custom rooted in antiquity. **Le fascina el antiguo Egipto.** He is enthralled by ancient Egypt.)

Antique, Antiquity, Antics. Palabras inglesas que suenan parecidas pero son muy distintas. *Antique* derivada del francés y *antics* del italiano *antico* en la acepción de *grotesco.* (**The antiques store had unique ítems on sale.** La tienda de antigüedades tenía en venta ejemplares únicos.) (**The teacher claimed that the study of antiquity helps us understand modern times.** El professor pretendía que el estudio de la antigüedad nos ayuda a comprender los tiempos modernos.) *Antics* puede traducirse como *travesuras, payasadas* o *comportamiento singular.* (**The baby's antics amused everyone.** A todos divirtieron las ocurrencias del bebé.)

Anunciante. *Anunciante* is whoever makes an announcement, more specifically an *advertiser* using a paper or magazine. (**El anunciante pagó el suplemento.** The advertiser paid for the supplement.)

Announcer. *Announcer* (*locutor* en español) se solía llamar *speaker* o *broadcaster.* (**Radio announcers pronounce foreign names correctly.** Los locutores pronuncian correctamente los nombres extranjeros.)

APARENTE. In Spanish, *aparente* means only *seeming*. (**Un aparente choque resultó ser un atentado.** What looked like a crash was actually an attack.)

APPARENT. Curiosamente, esta palabra inglesa puede querer decir tanto *aparente*, como lo contrario, *evidente*. Para ser preciso, en inglés habrá que decir *seeming* u *obvious*. (**It became apparent that he was not capable of doing that.** Resultó evidente que no era capaz de hacerlo.)

APASIONADO. *Passionate* may be a healthy emotion or one dominated by rage, but the Spanish usage tends to point to the former. (**Defensor apasionado de la justicia.** Passionate advocate of justice.)

PASSIONATE. *Passionate*, además de *apasionado* (**A passionate embrace.** Un abrazo apasionado.), significa *irascible, colérico*. (**After being contradicted, he became passionate with rage.** Tras ser contradicho, montó en cólera.)

APELACIÓN. There are two common meanings for *apelación*: a *designation*, a *name*; and an *appeal* before a court. (**Una apelación corriente.** A designation commonly used. **Su apelación fue aceptada.** His appeal was successful.)

APPELLATION, APPEAL. *Appeal* puede significar *recurso, apelación*, y también *llamamiento, exhortación*. (**The hostages' mother made an appeal to the kidnappers.** La madre de los rehenes dirigió un llamamiento a los captores.) *Appellation* significa *sobrenombre, mote*. (**He was known by the appellation "The big boss."** Se lo conocía por el sobrenombre "El gran patrón.")

APLICACIÓN. This is one of the most common Spanish deviations, to use *aplicar* or *aplicación* instead of *solicitar* or *solicitud*, when seeking employment, a grant, insurance, etc. In fact, *aplicación* is the use of some means for a treatment, or an effort in the performance of a job or study. (**El enfermo recibió una aplicación de rayos.** They gave the patient radiation treatment. **Por su aplicación, lo premiaron en la escuela.** His zeal earned him a prize in school.)

APPLICATION. Queda dicho que *application* es *petición, solicitud, postulación*. (**He filled out an application for the post.** Rellenó una solicitud para el cargo.) El papel en que se concreta la solicitud puede llamarse *formulario* (*form* en ingles).

APLICAR. Same as the previous entry.

APPLY. *Apply* recoge el mismo sentido indicado.

APOLOGÍA. *Apología* is defined by the Spanish Royal Academy as a *speech in defense or commendation* of someone or something. (**Es famosa la apología de Sócrates.** Socrates' apology has become famous.)

APOLOGY. *An apology* es también una *disculpa, una excusa.* (**After his comments, an apology was in order.** Después de lo que dijo, debía ofrecer disculpas.)

APROXIMAR. These are words of Latin origin, *approach* brought from the French *approche.* The common idea is that of *coming nearer. Aproximar* and *approximate* have common meanings, but I thought it interesting to point out some uses of *approach.*

APPROACH. *Approach* quiere decir *acercamiento, aproximación.* Significa también *enfoque, método, procedimiento.* (**You have to make a sensible approach to your boss if you want a raise.** Tienes que emplear un método razonable ante tu jefe para lograr un aumento.) *To approach* se traduce mejor por *encarar, plantear, considerar.* (**They approached the elements of the plan one by one.** Abordaron uno a uno los elementos del plan.) Lo que no le quita el elemento de aproximación, para la maniobra de acercamiento a un aeropuerto, por ejemplo. (**An ICAO manual deals with the approach maneuvres.** Un manual de la OACI trata las maniobras de aproximación.)

ÁREA. *Área* has become a common anglicism for *zona, región,* although it is risky because it also means an *are,* a metric unit of area equal to 100 square meters.

AREA. *Area* es una *región,* una *zona.* (**The city is in a very dry area.** La ciudad está en una región muy seca.)

ARENA. Originally used in reference to a circus, a bullfight *ruedo,* this word is more often used in the sense of *field, scene.* (**Su arena preferida eran los cafés.** Coffee houses were his preferred arena.)

ARENA. En español se usa esta palabra para sustituir a *liza, circo* o *ruedo,* como se dijo a la izquierda. (**The United Nations was the arena for bitter political debates.** Las Naciones Unidas fueron el escenario de amargos debates políticos.)

ARGÜIR. *Argüir* means *to put forth arguments, to discuss.* (**La esposa arguyó que un vecino la había amenazado.** The wife argued that a neighbor threatened her.)

ARGUE. *To argue* es *discutir, impugnar, disputar* una razón o argumento. (**The prosecutor argued against the reasoning of the defense.** El fiscal impugnó el razonamiento de la defensa.)

ARGUMENTO. The Spanish word refers to the *plot* or *script* of a literary or political work. (**El argumento de la película era muy enrevesado.** The film's plot was very convoluted.)

ARGUMENT. En inglés, se aplica esta palabra a una *disputa, discusión* o *controversia.* (**They engaged in a heated argument.** Se enzarzaron en una acalorada discusión.)

ARMADA. A curious difference in meaning: *armada* refers to the navy (the *Invincible Armada* for instance), while *army* is the land-based armed force.

ARMY. *Army*, por lo tanto, es *ejército.* (**The U.S. Army has bases in Europe and Asia.** El Ejército de los Estados Unidos tiene bases en Europa y en Asia.)

ARREGLAR. No particular differences between Spanish and English. The most common use of *arreglar* is *to fix.*

ARRANGE. Además de todo aquello que puede traducirse por arreglar, reparar, acomodar, etc., *to arrange* quiere decir *tomar disposiciones o providencias,* preparar las cosas para hacer algo, *organizar.* (**The organization arranged for a meeting to take place in April.** La organización tomó las disposiciones para reunirse en abril.)

ASALTO. *Asalto* may be a *round of a boxing match.* (**Terminó el combate noqueándolo en el tercer asalto.** The match was ended by a knockout in the third round.)

ASSAULT. El contexto indicará si *assault* se traduce por *ataque* o *agresión.* (**Assaulting a transportation employee is punishable as an assault against a police officer.** El ataque a un trabajador del transporte se castiga como el ataque a un agente de policía.)

ASAMBLEA. In Spanish, *asamblea* is *a meeting of people.*

ASSEMBLY. En inglés, *assembly* también quiere decir *montaje, armado* de un producto fabricado en piezas. (**Many labor-intensive articles have assembly shops in India and China.** Muchos artículos que exigen mucha mano de obra se montan en la India y China.)

ASCENDENCIA, ASCENDIENTE. *Ascendencia* is the *origin*, the *ancestry.* (**Pretende ser de ascendencia noble.** He claims to be of noble origin.) It can also be translated as *descent.* (**Es de ascendencia polaca.** He is of Polish descent.) *Ascendiente* means *influence, reputation.* (**El médico local tiene gran ascendiente en su pueblo.** The local doctor enjoys great influence in his village.)

ASCENDANCY. *Ascendancy* es una *influencia decisiva*, determinante. (**His ascendancy over the electorate is unchallenged.** Nadie disputa su influencia sobre el electorado.)

ASESINO. In Spanish, *asesino* is a *killer* or *murderer* who kills by any means. (**El asesino adujo motivos politicos.** The murderer said he was guided by political motives.)

ASSASSIN. El inglés ha retenido en el uso la acepción de *asesino* derivada del árabe hachischin, *el asesino a sueldo* a quien se preparaba embriagándolo de hachís. (**Those murders were the work of assassins employed by corrupt politicians.** Los crímenes fueron cometidos por asesinos a sueldo, contratados por políticos corruptos.)

ASISTENCIA. *Asistencia* is the *attendance* at a school or a meeting. But it is also *help*, synonymous with *ayuda*. The primary medical emergency service is called *asistencia pública* in Latin American countries. (**El concierto tuvo una asistencia entusiasta.** There was an enthusiastic attendance at the concert.)

ASSISTANCE. *Assistance* quiere decir *ayuda*, y no debe confundirse con *asistencia,* que se traduce por *attendance*. (**With the assistance of his wife, he established himself as a businessman.** Con la ayuda de su mujer, se estableció como empresario.)

ASISTIR. The verb *asistir* means to *be present*, *to attend*. (**Asistió al partido.** He attended the game.)

ASSIST. *To assist* es *ayudar*, como indica la palabra tratada anteriormente. (**The researcher was assisted in his experiment by a young graduate.** Un joven diplomado ayudó al investigador en sus experimentos.)

ASPERSIÓN. In both languages, the meaning is *to irrigate*. (**Se realiza este cultivo por aspersión.** This crop is cultivated by sprinkling.)

ASPERSION. Pero en inglés la acepción más común es la de *calumnia, difamación*. (**He cast aspersions on his enemy.** Difamó a su enemigo.)

ASUMIR. *Asumir* is to *take up a position, an obligation,* or *responsibilities.* Modern usage also coincides with the English meaning of *assume, being aware.* (**Asumió el cargo en una ceremonia especial.** He took office in a special ceremony.)

ASSUME. *To assume* es *dar por entendido, partir de un supuesto.* (**He assumed that he would be paid for his work.** Dio por sentado que le pagarían su trabajo.)

ATENDER. *To pay attention, to take care* of a person are the usual meanings. (**Atendió enseguida al enfermo.** He immediately took care of the patient.)

ATTEND. *To attend* quiere decir *asistir.* (**He attended the lecture and paid good attention to what was said then.** Asistió a la conferencia y atendió bien lo que entonces se dijo.)

ATENTADO, ATENTAR. *Atentado* is *an attempt to cause grave injury* to a person, generally in authority, or even the very fact of the *aggression.* (**En Iraq eran diarios los atentados.** In Iraq there were daily attacks against policemen.)

ATTEMPT. Del ejemplo de la columna anterior se ve claramente el uso de la palabra inglesa *attempt* en este sentido. Por supuesto se usa *attempt* en su acepción original de *intentar* o *tratar.* (**That was a failed attempt to convince him.** Fue un vano intento de convencerlo.)

AUDICIÓN. *Audición* is *the sense of hearing,* and also a *radio program or show,* since there is audio but not video. (**La audición consistió en dos entrevistas.** There were two interviews in the radio program.)

AUDITION. Se llama *audition* a una *prueba de selección* para el teatro o el cine. (**In the search for novel artists, the producers organized auditions.** Buscando artistas noveles, los productores organizaron pruebas de selección.)

AUDIENCIA. A *hearing*, set by an authority, a judge, etc. to discuss a proposal or to give testimony in a suit, is called *audiencia*. (**Antes de tomar alguna decision importante, el Ayuntamiento convoca a una audiencia popular.** Before making a major decision, the municipality arranges for a public hearing.)

AUDIENCE. *Audience* es el *público* de un espectáculo, conferencia o programa radial o televisivo. (**There is a service that measures the relative audience of TV shows, as a means of setting advertising rates.** Hay un servicio que mide el público de los programas televisivos, como medio de fijar las tarifas de publicidad.)

AUTO. Apart from being an abbreviation for *automobile*, *auto* has legal meanings in Spanish: a *judicial decision* or the *proceedings in a suit*. (**El testimonio figura en autos.** The witness statement is part of the proceedings. **El juez dictó auto de prisión contra el acusado.** The judge decided to send the accused to prison.) The same word designates a *play on Biblical or generally religious themes*. And *auto de fe* was the decision of the Spanish Tribunal of the Inquisition. As a prefix, *auto* can be translated as *self* (*autoservicio*, self-service).

AUTO. El prefijo *auto* puede entrar en la composición de muchas palabras en inglés en el sentido de *propio* (**autobiography**, autobiografía) o de propulsión o funcionamiento no asistido (**automatic break**, freno automático).

AUTORIDAD. There is no real difference between the two languages. In some cases, *officials* or *government* may be substituted for *autoridad*. (**Las autoridades fijaron nuevos impuestos.** The government established new taxes.)

AUTHORITY. Según el contexto, *authority* puede querer decir *autorización, jurisdicción o competencia*, especialmente para incurrir en un gasto. (**The manager had authority to spend up to a certain limit.** El gerente estaba autorizado a gastar hasta cierto límite.)

AVISAR. The Spanish word means *to warn*, *to announce*. (**Le avisó de su llegada.** He announced his arrival.)

ADVISE. *To advise* es *aconsejar*, no avisar. (**The ministers advise the president.** Los ministros aconsejan al presidente.) *Be advised* significa *sepa que*.

AZAR. *Azar* is *an event totally dependent on chance, coincidence, fortune. Al azar* is rendered *at random.* (**El nuevo dirigente se escogió al azar.** The new leader was chosen at random.)

HAZARD. *Hazard* quiere decir *riesgo, peligro.* (**Hazard in the job calls for extra pay.** Cuando el trabajo entraña riesgos, debe pagarse una prima.)

BACHILLER. *Bachiller* in Spanish usually means he who has completed secondary school. For the first level of university, *bachiller/bachelor (of arts, sciences, etc.)* is also used in both languages.

BACHELOR. *Bachiller (en artes, humanidades, ciencias, etc.)* suele referirse al primer grado de estudios universitarios. Además, en inglés *bachelor* quiere decir *soltero.* (**He is a confirmed bachelor.** Es un soltero impenitente.)

BALANCE. In bookkeeping, *balance* is understood as *balance sheet.* (**El balance de este año arrojó ganancias.** The balance sheet showed profit this year.)

BALANCE. Hay dos significados de *balance* que vale la pena retener: *equilibrio* y *saldo.* (**A balance between heart and brain.** El equilibrio entre el corazón y el cerebro. **Balance due is payable upon request.** El saldo de la deuda ha de pagarse a solicitud.)

BALOMPIÉ, BALONCESTO, BALONMANO. Although we are not dealing with false friends, this is an interesting matter to note. In Spain, hispanicized versions of the English words for different sports were invented: *balompié* for *football* (or *soccer*, known as *fútbol* elsewhere), *baloncesto*, for *basketball* (*básquetbol*), and *balonmano* (for *handball*). *Tennis* lost an *n* (*tenis*), *baseball* became *béisbol* (*juego de pelota* in Cuba), and other sports kept their original spelling: *squash*, *lacrosse*, etc.

-BALL. Aparte de las versiones hispanizadas que se citan en la otra columna, vale la pena notar que existe el *football* inglés, difundido en casi todo el mundo, y conocido en los Estados Unidos como *soccer* y la variante estadounidense, a la que se alude en español como *fútbol americano*. Sería largo enumerar las suertes o faltas de los distintos deportes, que han hallado una versión fonética del original inglés o traducción especial: *penalti, jonrón, saque*, etc.

BALÓN. *Balón* is a *ball* like the one used in soccer. (**El balón responde al reglamento.** The ball complies with regulations.)

BALLOON. *Balloon* es un *globo inflable*. (**After the victory, many balloons filled the air of the stadium.** Después del triunfo, muchos globos llenaron el cielo del estadio.)

BAR. In Spanish the meaning is simply an *establishment in which drinks are served*. (**Un bar para solteros.** A singles bar.)

BAR. En inglés *bar* tiene varios significados: *compás musical, barra de chocolate, código de barras, barrote de una cárcel* y, el que más nos interesa, el *Colegio de Abogados*. (**After successfully completing his graduate studies, he passed the bar exam.** Después de terminar sus estudios de posgrado, aprobó el examen del Colegio de Abogados.)

BARRIO. Although these are words of different origin (***barrio*** comes from Arabic and *borough* from old German), they have similar pronunciations and meanings. But ***barrio*** means *neighborhood*, *area*, or *zone*. (**Es un barrio de interés histórico.** It is a landmark neighborhood.)

BOROUGH. *Borough* es una *división administrativa*, que podría corresponder a *distrito*, pero no a *barrio*. (**New York City has five boroughs.** La ciudad de Nueva York tiene cinco distritos.)

BIGOTE. This pair appear to be of the same French origin, but have completely different meanings. ***Bigote*** is a *moustache*. (**Es extraño, pero Archie no tenía bigote.** Strangely enough, Archie did not have a moustache.)

BIGOT. Se dice del *intolerante*, *prejuiciado*. (**The defeated politician was a known bigot.** El politico derrotado era un intolerante conocido.)

BILLÓN. The Spanish Royal Academy describes ***billón*** as ***millón de millones*** (1,000,000,000,000).

BILLION. En los Estados Unidos se entiende por ***billion*** *mil millones*. (**A billion dollars is written $1,000,000,000.** Se expresa un billón de dólares con la cifra $1.000.000.000.)

BIZARRO. *Bizarro* is *gallant*, *courageous*, *magnanimous*. (**En la literatura clásica española se encuentran muchos caballeros bizarros.** Many gallant knights can be found in classical Spanish literature.)

BIZARRE. *Bizarre*, por su parte, denota algo muy distinto: *raro*, *extravagante*, *inhabitual*. (**Her bizarre actions were the first sign of mental illness.** Sus actitudes extravagantes fueron el primer indicio de su enfermedad mental.)

BONANZA. The original meaning of the Spanish word was restricted to *calm at sea*. (**El velero pasó por una zona de bonanza al segundo día.** The sailboat encountered an area of calm the second day.) But the English sense of *source of wealth* or *lucrative business* was later incorporated into Spanish.

BONANZA. *Bonanza* significa en ingles *veta de riqueza, mina* o *negocio lucrativo.* (**The stock exchange bonanza ended with the increase in oil prices.** El auge financiero de la bolsa terminó con el aumento de los precios del petróleo.)

BRAVO. There are similar meanings for these two words, but some particular ones deserve to be highlighted: *toro bravo (de lidia)* for the one engaged in bullfight, or *corrida*; and *torrential* or *rough*, like in *río Bravo*, on the Mexican-U.S. border, or *Costa Brava* on the Spanish Mediterranean.

BRAVE. *To brave* significa *capear, afrontar un clima o situación difícil.* (**The boat braved the storm.** El barco capeó el temporal.) También quiere decir *valiente, esforzado.* (**He was brave in adversity.** Se portó valerosamente ante la adversidad.)

BUFETE. *Bufete* is an *office*, particularly that of a solicitor or a notary. (**El abogado tenía su bufete en un rascacielos.** The lawyer had his office in a skyscraper.)

BUFFET. *Buffet* es la palabra francesa que pasó al inglés y al español para designar una mesa surtida de alimentos y no una cena formal. (**Lunch consisted of an assorted buffet.** El almuerzo consistió en un buffet surtido.)

CABALLERESCO. *Caballeresco* is what is characteristic of a gentleman, a *caballero* in Spanish. (**Sus gestos caballerescos le valieron la simpatía de todos.** His gentlemanly manners had him highly appreciated by everyone.)

CAVALIER. A menudo *cavalier* quiere decir *arrogante, altivo.* (**The salesman dismissed her complaint in a cavalier manner.** El vendedor descartó su queja de manera arrogante.) Curiosamente, aunque con menor frecuencia, también puede ser *galante, caballeresco.*

CÁLCULO. In Spanish *cálculo* means *a stone*. (**Le quitaron un cálculo renal.** He had a kidney stone removed.)

CALCULUS. *Calculus* es el título de la asignatura *cálculo matemático*. (**Calculus was a key subject in the auditing career.** El cálculo matemático era una materia clave en la carrera de auditor.)

CALIFICACIÓN, CUALIFICACIONES. *Calificaciones* is the word used in Spanish for *grades* (*notas escolares*). (**El boletín de calificaciones mostraba notas excepcionales.** The performance card showed exceptional grades.)

QUALIFICATION. *Qualifications* son *reservas, salvedades, limitaciones*. (**The country accepted the covenant without qualifications.** El país aceptó el pacto sin reservas. **He had excellent qualifications for the job.** Tenía excelentes cualificaciones para el puesto.)

CALIFICADO, CUALIFICADO. *Mayoría cualificada* is one that complies with the number of votes required by the rules. (**En ese caso se requería una mayoría cualificada.** In that situation a qualified majority was required.)

QUALIFIED. *To qualify* es *tener derecho, llenar las condiciones*, ser competente, para algo. (**He qualified for a social security bonus.** Tenía derecho a un premio del seguro social.)

CALLOSO. *Calloso* is simply someone who has a callus (*callo*). (**Por calloso no camina bien.** Because of his callus he has trouble walking.)

CALLOUS. Es *callous* un *perverso*, un *desalmado*. (**More than insensitive, he was callous.** Más que insensible, era un desalmado.)

CAMPAMENTO, CAMPO.
Campamento is translated as *camp*. (**A los niños les encanta ir a un campamento durante parte de sus vacaciones.** Children love to go to camp for part of their holidays.) *Campo*, for its part, is translated as *country* or *farm*. (**Las vacaciones en el campo se han vuelto muy populares últimamente.** Country holidays have become very popular recently.) It also means a *field* or *stadium*. (**el campo de fútbol del Barcelona**/Barcelona's soccer stadium) Or it can mean *field study*. (**La investigación comprendía un trabajo de campo.** The research included field study.)

CAMP. *Camp* nunca es *campo* sino *campamento*. (**The children's camp they preferred is in the countryside.** El campamento infantil que prefieren se halla en la campaña.)

CÁNDIDO. In Spanish, *cándido* has retained its original meaning: *naïve*. (**No se puede ser cándido en negocios.** In business, you cannot be naive.)

CANDID. *Candid* se utiliza con mayor frecuencia en sentido figurado, como sinónimo de *franco, sin tapujos*. (**Instead of using diplomatic language, the delegate spoke candidly.** En lugar de usar lenguaje diplomático, el delegado habló con franqueza.)

CARÁCTER. *Carácter* is *manuscript writing*, a *typeface* or a given *alphabet*. (**Escribió su nombre en caracteres cirílicos.** He wrote his name in the Cyrillic alphabet. **Dibuja caracteres regulares.** He writes with well-formed characters.)

CHARACTER. Sin contar el sentido habitual de *temperamento*, hay otras acepciones del inglés *character*. Empezando por *personaje*. (**Pirandello wrote a play "Six characters in search of a playwright."** Pirandello escribió la obra "Seis personajes en busca de un autor.") De manera peyorativa: **"What a character!"** ¡Qué tipejo!

CARBÓN, CARBONO. *Carbón* is rendered in English as *coal*. *Carbono* is the chemical element called *carbon* in English. (**Se usa el carbono 14 para determinar la antigüedad.** Carbon 14 is used to determine age.)

CARBON. El *carbón* es el artículo que en inglés se traduce por **coal**. (**Coal is used less and less for heating.** Se usa cada vez menos el carbón para calefacción.) *Carbon* es el elemento químico llamado *carbono* en español. (**Carbon 14 is used to determine age.** Se usa el carbono 14 para determinar la antigüedad.)

CARGA. *Carga* is *load*. (**La carga excedía el peso permitido.** There was a load in excess of the allowed weight.) It is also used in the sense of a *personal obligation* or *responsibility*. (**El cuidado del padre era una pesada carga.** His father's care was a heavy charge.)

CARGO, CHARGE. En un medio de transporte, particularmente el aéreo, *cargo* es la *carga* o *flete*. (**Air cargo rates have become affordable.** Las tarifas de carga aérea resultan hoy abordables.)

CARNAVAL. The pagan-Christian celebration of *carnaval* is known as *Mardi-Gras*, taking a part for the whole. (**En los Estados Unidos, el carnaval se festeja sobre todo en Nueva Orleáns.** In the U.S. Mardi Gras is celebrated mainly in New Orleans.)

CARNIVAL. *Carnival* ha pasado a ser *feria* o *parque de diversiones*. (**The village celebration included a carnival for children.** Los festejos locales incluían una feria para niños.)

CARTÓN. *Cartón* adopted the English meaning of *a case of...* but the original meaning is that of *cardboard*. (**El producto frágil estaba protegido por un envase de cartón.** The fragile article was protected by cardboard packaging.)

CARTON, CARTOON. *Cartoon* es algo muy diferente de *cartón*: un *dibujo animado*. (**Walt Disney was the master of the cartoon.** Walt Disney fue el maestro del dibujo animado.)

CASI, CUASI-. *Casi* is the equivalent of *almost*. *Cuasi-* is a prefix denoting something that does not include all the elements of the parent word, for instance *cuasicontrato* or *cuasidelito*, whose effects differ, albeit slightly in some cases, from *contrato*, *delito*, etc.

QUASI-. En inglés, se forman palabras con el prefijo *quasi-*, con el sentido de *aparente*, *parcialmente*, hasta cierto punto o con cierto parecido con el objeto especificado. (**A quasi-stellar body is a quasar or similar astronomical body.** Un objeto cuasiestelar es un quasar u otro objeto astronómico similar.)

CASUAL. In Spanish, something *casual* is the *result of chance and not of planning*, never, as in English, the opposite of *formal*. (**Fue un encuentro casual.** It was a chance meeting.)

CASUAL. En inglés, *casual* es lo opuesto de *formal*. (**Come as you are, attire is casual.** Venga como esté, no se requiere ropa formal.)

CASUALIDAD. *Casualidad* is an *unplanned event*, a *coincidencia*, something happening by chance. (**Dio la casualidad de que los dos eran graduados de la misma Universidad.** Coincidentally, both had graduated from the same university.)

CASUALLY, CASUALTY. Decir algo *casually* es *de pasada, sin pensarlo*, como quien no quiere la cosa. (**He spoke casually of his family.** Habló de su familia sin ceremonias.) *Casualty* es una *baja de guerra* y también el servicio de *urgencia de un hospital*. (**Casualties were numerous since the battle was fierce.** Hubo muchas bajas porque la batalla fue dura.)

CHARLATÁN. A *charlatán* in Spanish is someone who talks rather a lot, who is *talkative*. (**Es un charlatán divertido.** He chats in an entertaining way.)

CHARLATAN, CHAT. En inglés, el uso de esta voz se reserva al *embaucador*, al *curandero* u otro presunto conocedor de alguna materia que engaña con su labia, no al mero conversador. (**He claimed to be an innovative homeopathic doctor, but he was nothing more than a charlatan.** Pretendía ser un homeópata innovador, pero no era sino un embaucador.) Dicho sea de paso, *chat* es la palabra para *charla*. (**The chat was informative and entertaining.** La charla fue informativa y entretenida.)

CHOCOLATE. *Chocolate* designates the cocoa-based material and the delicacies manufactured with it. (**Belgas y suizos pretenden ambos haber inventado el chocolate.** The Belgians as well as the Swiss claim they invented chocolate.) To differentiate, the sweet is called *bombón* in some countries.

CHOCOLATE. Esta palabra designa no sólo la materia prima sino también la golosina que con ella se fabrica. *Chocolates* se usa para designar las golosinas hechas con este producto. (**He is addicted to chocolates after dinner.** Tiene el vicio de los chocolates después de la cena.)

CIFRAS. There are differences in how figures are expressed in English and Spanish. The decimal point becomes a comma in Spanish (1.000,00 versus 1,000.00). And the Spanish point used to separate thousands and millions becomes a comma in English (1,000,000,000). *See also* **Fechas**, **Horas**.

FIGURES. Hay algunas diferencias con la manera de expresar cifras en inglés. Para las cantidades de enteros y decimales, se usa el punto donde en español iría la coma y viceversa (1,000.00). Para cifras inferiores a la unidad, en inglés puede no ponerse el cero (.76 en lugar de 0,76). Popularmente, se llama *buck* al dólar, *grand* a mil dólares, y suelen darse precios con *k*, para significar miles, *m*, millones, y *b*, billones.

CÍNICO. Originally, this word referred to a philosophical school of Ancient Greece, but now it has the common meaning of *insincere, brazen*.

CYNICAL. La acepción original, similar a la del español, cede en inglés ante la idea de *sarcástico, capcioso*. (**He made a cynical remark.** Hizo una observación capciosa.)

CIRCO. *Circo* can be another word for *arena*. (**El "pan y circo" de César se refería a la buena comida y los gladiadores en el circo.** Caesar's "bread and circus" referred to good food and the gladiators in the arena.)

CIRCUS. En el famoso sitio *Picadilly Circus*, la voz se aplica a una plaza circular, aunque en el uso no se ha extendido a una *rotonda* o *glorieta*, para la que se usa en Gran Bretaña el *roundabout* o, como se decía antes, *rondpoint*.

CIRCULANTE, CIRCULACIÓN.
The *currency* that circulates
in a country is *circulante*.
(**El circulante aumentó con
la inflación.** The money in
use increased with inflation.)
Circulación is *traffic*, and also can
refer to *circulación de la sangre*
(blood circulation).

CIRCULATION. Más bien que
circulación, **circulation** se
refiere a la *tirada* vendida de
un periódico. (**The American
Bureau of Circulation checks the
circulation of a paper.** La Oficina
de Circulación de los Estados
Unidos verifica la tirada vendida
de un periódico.)

CIRCULAR. In Spanish, *circular*
is a general way of saying *to
move by different conveyances*.
(**En Inglaterra, se circula por la
izquierda.** Traffic moves on the
left in England.)

CIRCULATE. En su forma transitiva,
este verbo significa *distribuir,
difundir, repartir*. (**At the United
Nations the rules determine that
documents should be circulated
simultaneously in the six official
languages.** En las Naciones
Unidas el reglamento dispone
que los documentos deben ser
distribuidos simultáneamente en
los seis idiomas oficiales.)

CLERICAL. In Spanish,
clerical means only related
to *clero, the clergy*. (**Los
izquierdistas organizaron
manifestaciones anti-clericales.**
Left-wingers organized
anticlerical demonstrations.)

CLERICAL. Los empleados de
oficina desempeñan tareas
que se definen como *clerical*.
(**Clerical jobs are paid the
minimum wage.** Los empleados
de oficina no especializados
reciben el salario mínimo.)

COLEGIO, ESCUELA, INSTITUTO.
Usage is the determining factor in
every country. In some countries,
colegio is a high school that
trains students in commercial or
technical crafts, while *escuela* is
just a *preparation for college or
university*. In Spain, *instituto* is
usually *high school*.

COLLEGE, SCHOOL. Se designa
como *college* a un centro
de enseñanza dentro de una
universidad o a la universidad
misma. La educación secundaria
se imparte en Estados Unidos en
junior high school seguida de
high school.

COLLAR, CUELLO. *Collar* may
mean *necklace*. *Cuello* means *neck*.
(**Lucía llevó un collar de perlas.**
Lucia wore a pearl necklace. **Un
fino cuello distinguido.** A fine
distinguished neck.)

COLLAR. *Cuello* y el *collar* de un
perro se designan con la palabra
inglesa *collar*. (**From the dog's
collar hung the registration and
vaccination plaques.** Del cuello
del perro pendían las placas de
registro y vacunas.)

COMERCIAL. *Comercial* is
something related to commerce
or trade. (**La balanza comercial
mejoró este año.** This year, the
trade balance improved.)

COMMERCIAL. Se llama
commercial en Estados Unidos a
un *anuncio publicitario*. (**There
are too many commercials on
TV.** Hay exceso de anuncios
publicitarios en la TV.) Pero
también se usa en la acepción
relacionada con el comercio.

COMETER. Only the meaning
of *to carry out (a crime,
etc.)* is retained from the
original meaning of *cometer*.
(**Cometió un grave error.** He
committed a big mistake.)

COMMIT. Además de llevar a cabo
to commit quiere decir *recluir*,
en el caso de reos, ancianos o
enfermos. (**Since he suffered from
Alzheimer's, he was committed
to an institution.** Como
padecía el mal de Alzheimer,
se lo recluyó en un asilo.)

COMIENZO. In Spanish, the only meaning of *comienzo* is *a beginning*.

COMMENCEMENT. *Commencement* es la *ceremonia de graduación universitaria*, curiosamente al final de los estudios. Presumiblemente alude al comienzo de la vida profesional, ya que los graduados se definen como *class of...* (el año de graduación y no del comienzo de las clases). (**Commencement is at the same time a solemn and joyous occasion.** La graduación es al mismo tiempo una ocasión solemne y alegre.)

COMISIÓN, COMITÉ. Words totally synonymous, the choice depending on nonsemantic preferences. It is possible to describe as a *comisión* a gathering of all the members of an organization or company, while *comité* is reserved for a restricted body. *See also Session.*

COMMISSION, COMMITTEE. *Commission* y *committee* en la práctica son términos intercambiables.

COMODIDAD. *Comodidad* is *comfort* and, as we already saw, *amenity* also means *comodidad*, in the sense of the characteristics proper of an apartment or a house. (**El piso ofrece gran comodidad.** The apartment has many amenities.)

COMMODITY. *Commodities* son los bienes que se hallan en el comercio. En el uso de las Naciones Unidas, el uso se restringe específicamente a los productos básicos. (**Many developing countries depend on the market for their commodities, and the wide variation in prices could be catastrophic for their economies.** Muchos países en desarrollo dependen del mercado de sus productos básicos, y las amplias variaciones de precios pueden ser catastróficas para sus economías.)

CÓMODO. *Cómodo*, even in a figurative sense, is rendered by *comfortable*. (**Me siento cómodo en mi puesto.** I feel comfortable with my job.)

COMMODIOUS. En *commodious* es importante la idea de *amplio*, *espacioso*. (**A commodious living room was the main attraction of the apartment.** La principal atracción del apartamento era un amplísimo salón.)

COMPÁS. The many meanings of the word *compás* correspond to the English *compass*. In the expression *compás de espera*, borrowing a musical term, it means *a pause*. (**Se tomó un compás de espera antes de decidir.** He waited for a while before deciding.)

COMPASS. Muchos instrumentos reciben el nombre de *compass*, incluso la *brújula*, que se distingue de los demás por su designación específica. (**He was so lost he needed a compass to ascertain his location.** Estaba tan perdido que necesitaba una brújula para comprobar su situación.)

COMPLACENCIA. The Spanish term means *pleasure, satisfaction*. (**Contó con la complacencia de sus clientes.** His customers were satisfied.)

COMPLACENCY, COMPLACENT. Estos términos habitualmente se equiparan. Pero *complacency* ha adquirido un sentido casi peyorativo, al designar la *aquiescencia ciega*, sin impugnar lo negativo. (**We should not feel complacent with the state of the economy.** No deberíamos aceptar sin crítica la situación económica.)

COMPLEXIÓN. Two different meanings between the English and the Spanish terms. In Spanish it refers to *physical appearance, the body's strength*. (**Su complexión intimidaba.** His physical appearance intimidated.)

COMPLEXION. *Complexion* significa *tez, cutis*. (**The model had a beautiful complexion.** La modelo tenía un cutis perfecto.)

COMPOSITOR. A *music composer* is a *compositor*. (**Hay muchos compositores barrocos que empiezan a escucharse.** Many baroque composers are being heard now.)

COMPOSITOR, COMPOSER. *Compositor* es un término de imprenta: *cajista*. (**As papers are prepared with computers, compositors are as unemployed as telegraphists.** Como los periódicos se componen por ordenador, los cajistas están tan desocupados como los telegrafistas. **The orchestra played works of their conductor-composer.** La orquesta tocó obras de su director-compositor.)

COMPROMETER, COMPROMISO.
Comprometer means *to make an engagement*, but is widely employed now in the English sense to mean *to give in, to accept albeit reluctantly*. **Solución de compromiso** is very commonly used. Curiously, in a United Nations discussion there was talk of *el compromiso hallado para cumplir los compromisos acordados* (the compromise solution found so that the agreed engagements be respected).

COMPROMISE. El uso de *compromise solution* en el sentido de *solución de avenencia* o *transacción* es hoy moneda corriente en negociaciones internacionales o empresariales. (**A compromise solution does not completely satisfy each party.** Una solución de transacción no satisface del todo a ninguna de las partes.)

CONCLUIR. *Concluir* is simply *to finish something*. (**El acto concluyó puntualmente.** The ceremony ended on time.)

CONCLUDE. *To conclude* no es meramente concluir algo sino *llegar a conclusiones*. (**The Committee concluded that many reforms had to be undertaken.** El comité llegó a la conclusión de que había que emprender muchas reformas.)

CONCURRIR. *Concurrir* means *to attend*. (**Concurrió mucho público a la inauguración de la exposición.** Quite a large audience attended the inauguration of the show.)

CONCUR. *To concur* es *convenir, acordar algo, aprobar*. (**The members concurred with the President that another negotiating meeting was necessary.** Los miembros convinieron con el Presidente en que hacía falta una reunión negociadora más.)

CONDUCTA. *Conducta* is *conduct* or *behavior*. *Código de conducta* is the *code of ethics* of a profession or a company. (**Su conducta fue ejemplar.** He showed exemplary behavior.)

CONDUCT. La *dirección de un debate, de una orquesta o coro* es su **conduct**. (**His skill made his conduct of the discussion a success.** Su talento hizo que su dirección del debate fuera un éxito.) ·

CONDUCTOR. Whoever drives (*conduce*) a vehicle is a **conductor** (or *chofer*). (**Cada conductor debe respetar las reglas de la circulación.** Every driver must respect the traffic rules.)

CONDUCTOR. En el uso estadounidense (no así en el Reino Unido), *conductor* no es quien conduce el tren o el metro (*motorman* u *operator*) sino el *guardatrén* o *interventor*. (**The conductor travels in the sixth car of the subway.** El guardatrén viaja en el sexto vagón del metro.) Y, como ya señalamos, el director de orquesta.

CONFECCIÓN. *Confección* is *production, manufacture*, and is more specifically used for the garment industry, the manufacture of textiles; also as opposed to *made to measure*. (**Su traje de confección le sienta a maravilla.** His ready-made suit is a perfect fit.)

CONFECTION. Esta palabra se usa fundamentalmente para la *repostería o confitería*. (**French confections are preferred the world over.** La repostería francesa es preferida en todo el mundo.)

CONFECCIONISTA. *Confeccionista* is a *manufacturer of textiles*.

CONFECTIONER. *Confectioner* se traduce por *repostero*.

CONFETI. There is no difficulty understanding this word, which is used in English but is replaceable in Spanish.

CONFETTI. Esta es una de esas palabras que se han incorporado al español, ya que *papel picado* existe desde siempre.

CONFLICTO. In most cases, the meanings are equivalent. (**El conflicto del Medio Oriente lleva tiempo sin resolver.** The Middle East conflict has yet to be resolved.)

CONFLICT. El verbo *to conflict* quiere decir *estar en pugna, discordar.* (**His version of the facts conflicted with that of the police.** Su versión de los hechos discrepaba con la de la policía.)

CONFRONTACIÓN. Again, a word that has entered Spanish by the back door. *Confrontación* means *cotejo, comparison, verification.* But usage has equalled this word with *enfrentamiento.* (**La confrontación de ambos testimonios reveló diferencias.** The comparison of the two witnesses' stories revealed differences.) A word that can be sometimes used for *enfrentamiento* is *showdown.* (**El enfrentamiento resultó inevitable tras la disputa.** The showdown could not be avoided after their argument.)

CONFRONTATION. *Confrontation* conlleva la idea de *lucha, conflicto,* incluso armado. (**Instead of confrontation there should be negotiation.** En lugar del enfrentamiento, debería haber negociación.)

CONGELAR. The meaning of *congelar* is *to freeze.* (**Los productos congelados pueden almacenarse durante largos períodos.** Frozen goods can be stored for very long periods.)

CONGEAL. *To congeal* no es congelar sino *cuajarse, coagular.* (**Clots are the result of congealed blood.** Los coágulos son resultado de la coagulación de la sangre.)

Conjura, Conjuro. *Conjuro* is *an urging*, *a request*, without relation to *conjura,* a conspiracy. (**Al conjuro de su discípulo, el maestro accedió a repetir la demostración.** At the urging of the student, the professor agreed to repeat the demonstration.)

Conjure. *To conjure* es *invocar* (un recuerdo, el demonio, un espíritu). (**The speaker conjured the memory of his mentor.** El orador invocó la memoria de su mentor.)

Conmutar. From the Latin *commutare*, meaning *change*, *conmutar* refers to exchanging a penalty for one less severe. (**El Presidente conmutó la pena de muerte del reo por la de prisión perpetua.** The President commuted the convict's death penalty to a life sentence.)

Commutate, Commute. *To commute* significa, además del término jurídico de cambiar una pena por una menos grave, *viajar de la casa al trabajo*, por lo general situado a cierta distancia. (**From the suburbs, he commutes every day to the city.** Él viaja diariamente desde los suburbios a la ciudad.) *To commutate* es *cambiar el sentido de la corriente eléctrica.* (**Alternate current was commutated to direct current.** La corriente alterna se transformó en directa.)

Consecuencia. One of the meanings of *consecuencia* is *consistency.* (**Su consecuencia en la defensa de los derechos humanos es reconocida.** His consistency in the defense of human rights is well recognized.) *See* ***Consistencia.***

Consequence. *A person of consequence* es una persona de alto rango. Algo diferente de *a person of substance*, que significa alguien acaudalado, con fortuna. (**In his community, he was a person of consequence.** Era una persona de autoridad en su comunidad.)

CONSEJO. *Consejo* means *advice*. (**Siguió el consejo de su abogado.** He followed the advice of his lawyer.)

COUNSEL. *Counsel* es *abogado*. (**A detainee is entitled to counsel.** Un detenido tiene derecho a tener abogado.) También puede ser *aconsejar/asesorar* o *asesoramiento*. (**Corporation executives give counsel to new entrepreneurs.** Ejecutivos de grandes empresas aconsejan a nuevos empresarios.)

CONSERVATORIO. Both words are used for *school of music*, in Spanish almost exclusively with this meaning. (**El conservatorio ofreció un concierto de los recién diplomados.** There was a concert of recent graduates at the school of music.)

CONSERVATORY. En inglés se usa *conservatory* o *greenhouse* en el sentido de *invernadero*. (**The Arboretum housed a conservatory with rare species.** En el Arboretum había un invernadero con especies poco comunes.)

CONSIDERACIÓN. No specific problem with this pair of words.

CONSIDERATION. Hacer algo *for a consideration* quiere decir *mediante pago*. (**The ensemble agreed to play at the benefit for a modest consideration.** El conjunto aceptó actuar en el recital a beneficio por una reducida retribución.)

CONSISTENCIA. *Consistencia* is *firmness, solidity, hardness*. (**El mueble tiene una gran consistencia.** It is a very solid piece of furniture.)

CONSISTENCY, CONSISTENT. *Consistency* es *coherencia, correspondencia*. (**There is consistency between the two legal texts.** Hay coherencia entre los dos textos legales.) *To be consistent* significa *ser consecuente, coherente*. (**His conduct is consistent.** Tiene una actitud coherente.)

CONSPICUO. You become *conspicuo* if you are recognized because of your moral or formal authority. (**Es un miembro conspicuo de su comunidad.** He is a distinguished member of his community.)

CONSPICUOUS. *Conspicuous* es algo *llamativo*, fácil de reconocer por su aspecto o posición sobresaliente. (**In the crowd, he was conspicuous for his bright red hat.** En la multitud, él se destacaba por su brillante sombrero rojo.)

CONSTIPADO. Spanish deviated from English and French (that had this word derived from Latin, meaning *to confine the bowels, cram*), ending with the meaning, *a cold.* (**Todos los inviernos pesca un constipado.** Every year he gets a cold in winter.)

CONSTIPATION. *Estreñimiento* es el equivalente español de *constipation.* (**Laxatives can give relief from constipation.** Los laxantes pueden aliviar el estreñimiento.)

CONTEMPLAR. English influence is responsible for the use of *contemplar* in the sense of *consider.* (**Está contemplando veranear en una playa.** He plans to spend the summer at a beach resort.)

CONTEMPLATE. *To contemplate* se traduce por *prever, considerar, proponerse* o tener la intención de hacer algo. (**The President contemplated traveling to the war zone.** El Presidente pensó en viajar a la zona de guerra.)

CONTENTO. *Contento* means *happy.* (**Estaba loco de contento.** He was mad with joy.)

CONTEMPT. *Contempt* significa *desdén,* y como término jurídico o parlamentario, *desacato, rebeldía.* (**He was found in contempt of court.** Lo declararon en desacato al tribunal.)

CONTESTACIÓN. A noun derived from *contestar. (See below.)*

CONTESTATION. El sustantivo derivado de *to contest. Véase más abajo.*

CONTESTAR. In Spanish, *contestar* is almost always used in the sense of *to reply, to answer.* (**La defensa contestó los alegatos del fiscal.** The defense answered the prosecutor's allegations.)

CONTEST. Palabra con muchas acepciones: *disputar, impugnar, discutir,* y en su forma sustantiva, *concurso, certamen, debate, discusión.* (**The candidate contested the jury findings.** El candidato impugnó las conclusiones del jurado. **That was a difficult contest.** Fue un certamen muy difícil.)

CONVENIENCIA. English and Spanish meanings are essentially synonymous.

CONVENIENCE. *Convenience* puede ser un eufemismo para designar el *lavabo. Convenience stores* en los Estados Unidos son pequeñas tiendas que venden los artículos básicos: leche, pan, etc. (**The small village only had a convenience store; the market was 20 miles away.** La aldea sólo tenía una tienda básica; el mercado se hallaba a 20 millas de distancia.)

CONVENIR. *Convenir* means *to agree.* (**Convinimos en que revisaríamos el contrato.** We agreed we would review the contract.)

CONVENE. *To convene* significa *convocar* (una reunión, por ejemplo). (**A meeting with both parties was convened for arbitration.** Se convocó a ambas partes a una reunión de arbitraje.)

CONVERSADOR. He who chats in an entertaining, intelligent way is a *conversador.* (**Conversador ameno, divertía a la concurrencia.** An entertaining talker, he amused the audience.)

CONVERSANT. Se dice de quien que está familiarizado con una materia. (**The consultant is conversant with the new technique.** El consultor está familiarizado con la nueva técnica.)

CONVICCIÓN. *Convicción* is *certainty, firm belief.* (**El padre tenía la convicción de haber educado bien a su hijo.** The father was firmly convinced that he had given his son a good education.)

CONVICTION. *Conviction* es el hecho de declarar culpable a un acusado. (**After the conviction, the judge pronounced the sentence.** Tras declarar convicto al reo, el juez leyó la sentencia.)

COPIA. *Copia* is a mere *reproduction* of something. (**La copia resultó mejor que el original.** The copy was better than the original.)

COPY. A menudo se traduce *copy* por *copia* cuando debiera ser *ejemplar.* (**More than a million copies were sold of this book.** Se vendieron más de un millón de ejemplares de ese libro.)

CORREO ELECTRÓNICO. In popular parlance, it is common now in Spain and Latin America to talk of sending *a mail*, meaning *an e-mail*. However, the expression that now has the seal of approval of the Royal Academy is *correo electrónico*.

E-mail, evidentemente, es un intento absurdo de definir el e-mail. Cuando la Academia de la Lengua estaba abocada a elegir un término español, optó por *correo electrónico* entre varias posibilidades, entre las que se contaba *emilio*, por razones de eufonía. Solución no absurda, cuando se piensa que el signo @, que en español se dice *arroba*, emplea esta acepción para un fin totalmente distinto del original, medida de peso.

CORTE. Words that have several meanings, both in English and in Spanish. (**Hace la corte a su colega de oficina.** He courts his colleague at the office. **Las Cortes Catalanas duraron poco.** The Catalan Parliament did not last long.)

COURT. *Court* puede ser un *tribunal* o *un juzgado*. (**The International Criminal Court.** El Tribunal Penal Internacional. **The Kingdom of Spain has no apparent court.** No hay una corte ostensible en el Reino de España. **He lives at Grace Court in Brooklyn.** Vive en la callejuela Grace de Brooklyn.)

COSTUMBRE. *Costumbre* may be translated by *custom* or *practice*. (**La costumbre es ley.** Custom becomes the law. **Dar propina al camarero se ha vuelto costumbre.** It is customary to tip a waiter.)

CUSTOM, COSTUME. Utilizada como adjetivo, la palabra *custom* indica algo *hecho por encargo, a medida*, o por orden del comprador. (**He wears only custom-made shirts.** Sólo usa camisas hechas a medida.) *Costume* es *un traje*; la palabra se usa particularmente para los trajes nacionales y los de disfraz. (**The Korean bride wore a traditional costume for the ceremony.** La novia coreana vestía un traje tradicional para la ceremonia. **The celebration concluded with a costume ball.** Los festejos terminaron con un baile de disfraz.)

CREDENCIAL. A *credencial* is a *badge* that establishes the identity of the bearer. (**Tienes que mostrar tu credencial para el acceso al edificio.** You have to show your badge to gain access to the building.) *Cartas credenciales* are the powers given to a diplomat to exercise his functions.

CREDENTIAL. Por extensión del significado de *cartas credenciales*, *credentials* son los títulos o la experiencia que permiten a alguien ejercer su profesión u oficio. (**His years at the Ministry were sufficient credentials for his new job.** Los años que pasó en el Ministerio le dieron títulos suficientes para el nuevo cargo.)

CRÉDITO. *Crédito* may be a *loan* as well as the *reliability of a debtor,* sometimes measured in a currency amount. (**Su crédito era impecable.** He had impeccable credit.)

CREDIT. Entre los usos de esta palabra que no responden a las acepciones claras de crédito están *reconocimiento, mérito, motivo de orgullo* y también el *puntaje* atribuido a una materia, curso o actividad desarrollada con miras a la obtención de un título universitario. (**To her credit, she sacrificed her career caring for her parents.** Tuvo el gran mérito de haber sacrificado su carrera para atender a sus padres. **His life experience earned him several credits.** Por su experiencia obtuvo varios puntos.)

CRIMEN. The Spanish word, while defined as a *serious offense,* is also often used in the restricted sense of *killing* or seriously injuring someone. (**El crimen quedó impune.** The murder remained unsolved.)

CRIME. *Crime* significa *delito.* En la legislación de Estados Unidos, por ejemplo, hay una larga serie de acciones que pueden ser *felony, larceny, misdemeanor, manslaughter* de primer o segundo orden (*first or second degree*).

CRIMINAL. In Spanish, the word *criminal* is reserved for the perpetrator of serious crimes, notably murder, as a synonym of *asesino.*

CRIMINAL. *Criminal* puede querer decir simplemente *delincuente.* En *el Tribunal Penal Internacional,* se traduce por *The International Criminal Court.*

CRÍTICA, CRÍTICO. *Crítica* is the equivalent of *criticism*, although it may not be negative, and would then be rendered by *review*. (**La crítica teatral le fue favorable.** He had a favorable review of his play.) *Crítico* may be the *reviewer* or *critic*. (**Es el crítico teatral del New York Times.** He is the theater reviewer of the New York Times.)

CRITICISM, CRITICAL. Como adjetivo, *critical* puede significar *vital, decisivo, fundamental.* (**He appeared at the critical moment.** Apareció en el momento decisivo.)

CRUASÁN. Popular pastry of breakfast, the French word spelled with Spanish sounds has replaced the *media luna* common in many Latin American countries.

CROISSANT. En Latinoamérica a esta torta o pasta se la llama *media luna*, ya que no hay razón para tomar una voz francesa con el mismo sentido. En otra acepción de la voz francesa *croissant* o de la inglesa *crescent*, encontramos la Liga Internacional de Sociedades de la Cruz Roja y de la Media Luna Roja.

CUBIERTA, CUBIERTO, CUBRIR. *Cubierta* is the *cover* of a book or the *deck* of a boat. *Cubierto* is cutlery or place settings and the number of guests at a restaurant. (**Reservó dos cubiertos.** He made a reservation at the restaurant for two people.)

COVER. Además de *cubrir, to cover* se utiliza a menudo en el sentido de *abarcar, comprender, cobijar.* (**Her husband is covered by her insurance.** Su marido está comprendido en su seguro.) *No cover* en un restaurante o club nocturno significa que no se cobra cubierto o, en realidad, derecho de espectáculo. *Undercover agent* es *un espía u oficial de inteligencia.*

CUERPO. *Cuerpo* is just a *body*, in all its meanings. *Cadáver* is a *corpse*.

CORPSE. *Corpse* es *cuerpo*, pero sólo en el caso de uno inanimado, un *cadáver*. (**The film Black Orpheus showed a morgue full of corpses after the Rio carnival.** La película Orfeo Negro mostraba la morgue llena de cadáveres después del carnaval de Río.)

CURADOR, CURANDERO, CURATIVO. *Curador* is *one who cures*, but the word is seldom used. *Curativo* is *curative*, and *curandero* is a *healer*. (**En su desesperación ante su grave enfermedad, acudió al curandero.** In his desperation, the seriously ill man went to a healer.)

CURATOR. *Curator* es el *conservador* de un museo, de una de sus salas o de una galería. (**The curator of the Egyptian wing is an expert in mummies.** El conservador del ala egipcia es un experto en momias.)

CURIOSO. A seldom-used meaning of this word is *neat, tidy*, coming as it does, from the Latin *cura, care*. (**Es muy curioso si se trata de su ropa.** When it comes to his clothes, he is very neat.)

CURIOUS. *Curious*, igual que otras palabras tratadas en este glosario, se aplica muy a menudo con un sentido peyorativo. En este caso, puede traducirse como *indiscreto, minucioso, raro*. (**He is curious to the point of alienating people.** Su indiscreción le agencia la mala voluntad de la gente.)

DECAER. *Decaer* is *to decline, to become weaker*. (**Tenía aspecto decaído.** He had a weakened appearance.)

DECAY. *Decay* es algo más que *decaer*, implica *ruina, podredumbre, descomposición*. (**Tooth decay is fought with fluoride.** Se combate la caries dental con flúor. **The decay of the building was due to lack of maintenance.** La ruina del edificio se debía a falta de mantenimiento.)

DECENTE. As an opposite of *indecente*, **decente** does not raise any problem for the translator. But as we say in the right-hand column, *digno* can be a better choice.

DECENT. La Oficina Internacional del Trabajo ha venido promoviendo últimamente el llamado **decent work,** que la Oficina traduce a sus otros dos idiomas oficiales como *travail décent y trabajo decente*. Es evidente que las tres expresiones "homónimas" tienden a optimizar la campaña, pero el resultado en español, (y tal vez en los otros dos idiomas) no es muy feliz desde el punto de vista lingüístico. Lo correcto es hablar de trabajo, o empleo *digno* o *decoroso*.

DECEPCIÓN. The Spanish word means *disappointment*. (**La actitud de su amigo le produjo una gran decepción.** His friend's behavior was a big disappointment.)

DECEPTION. *Deception* es sinónimo de *engaño, impostura, superchería*. (**That scheme used deception to get recruits.** El plan se valió del engaño para conseguir adeptos.)

DECLINACIÓN, DECLINAR. *Declinar, declinación* convey the idea of *decay, of ruin*. (**Gorbachov precipitó la declinación del poder soviético.** Gorbachev precipitated the decline of Soviet power.)

DECLINE. *Decline* se usa como sinónimo de *renunciar, negarse a algo*. (**He was offered a new position, but he declined.** Le ofrecieron un nuevo cargo, pero no aceptó.) Término gramatical, usado para los distintos casos. (**Nouns are declined in Latin.** Los sustantivos se declinan en latín.)

DECRETAR. Nothing special to note with regard to the Spanish term, meaning *to establish by decree*.

DECREE. Hay un uso figurado de **decree**, por *decidir tiránicamente*. (**His mother decreed that he should become a lawyer.** Su madre decidió que él fuera abogado.)

DEDICAR. The main meaning of these words is the same. (**El deportista dedicó el triunfo a su madre.** The player dedicated the victory to his mother.)

DEDICATE. *To dedicate* puede ser algo más que *dedicarse*: *consagrarse* a alguien, *mostrar devoción* o prestar grandes cuidados. (**A dedicated staff made sure that the business venture became successful.** El personal consagrado a la tarea aseguró el éxito de la empresa comercial.)

DEFENDER. In its reflexive form, *defenderse* means *to do well, to have a good economic situation*. (**Ahora que tiene su propia empresa, se defiende bastante bien.** Now that he has his own company, he is in a good situation.)

DEFEND. *To defend a doctoral thesis* se traduce mejor por *sostener una tesis del doctorado*.

DEFENSOR. *Defensor* is a *defender*, the one who defends a thesis. (**La naturaleza tiene en esta organización a un firme defensor.** Nature has a strong defender in this organization.) *Abogado defensor* is *counsel for the defense*.

DEFENDANT, DEFENDER. *Defendant* es el *demandado* o acusado en un juicio. (**The defendant believed his counsel did not present his case adequately.** El demandado creyó que su abogado no había planteado su posición de modo apropiado.) *Defender* es quien defiende una causa. (**Human rights defenders risk their lives.** Los defensores de derechos humanos arriesgan sus vidas.)

DEFINIDO. *Definido* and *defined* are synonymous. (**Pintar los muros con grafitti se ha definido como delito.** Defacing walls with grafitti has been defined as a crime.)

DEFINITE(LY). *Definite* quiere decir *claramente determinado*, pero *definitely* no es *definitivamente* sino *decididamente, sin falta*. (**I will definitely attend the meeting.** Asistiré sin falta a la reunión.)

Delincuente. *Delincuente* ís generic for *criminal*, a term that in English has a wider range than in Spanish. (**En los Estados Unidos le leen al delincuente la lista de sus derechos, los "Miranda."** In the United States, each criminal is read his Miranda rights.)

Delinquent. Ya se ha visto que *delincuente* es *criminal*, no así *delinquent*, que califica al deudor *moroso* o a la *deuda vencida*. (**After 30 days of non-payment of a bill, the account is considered delinquent.** Después de 30 días, la factura impaga es considerada morosa.) En *juvenile delinquent* (*delincuente juvenil*) encontramos la acepción emparentada con el español.

Demanda. These words have similar meanings. *Demanda* is a legal term defining the purpose of a lawsuit. (**El proceso consistió en una demanda de indemnización.** The lawsuit was a claim for compensation.)

Demand. Se dice de un documento que es *on demand* si es pagadero a la vista o a la presentación. (**He presented a bill of exchange on demand.** Presentó una carta de crédito pagadera a la vista.)

Demostración. *Demostración* is a *show* or *proof* of the way something works. (**Hubo una demostración de vehículos todo terreno.** There was a show of four-wheel drive vehicles.)

Demonstration. En el uso de los Estados Unidos, además de la muestra del funcionamiento o eficiencia de algo, *demonstration* es *una manifestación*. (**Autocratic regimes do not tolerate popular demonstrations.** Los regímenes autocráticos no toleran las manifestaciones populares.)

DENOMINACIÓN. *Denominación* is *name* in Spanish. Under the influence of French, it is said of wines or special products, as regulated by the European Union. But more precise is *designación*, as in *designación de origen controlada* (*verified name of origin*).

DENOMINATION. El dinero corriente se distribuye en varias *denominations*, o *billetes de valores diferentes*. (**In the U.S., bills of every denomination are of the same size.** Los billetes de dólares de todos los valores tienen el mismo tamaño.) Hay iglesias cristianas de distintas *denominations*. (**There are several Christian churches of different denominations.** Hay varias iglesias cristianas de distinto *culto* [o *rito*, en algunos casos].) Si no, el traductor debería simplemente designar a cada una por su nombre: Iglesia Bautista, Episcopal, etc.

DENSO. No real difference in the original meaning of these words.

DENSE. Vale la pena notar el sentido negativo de *dense*: *torpe, estúpido, craso* (ignorante). (**He is dense beyond measure.** Es un tonto de capirote.)

DEPARTAMENTO. What is called an *apartment* or a *flat* becomes *departamento* or *apartamento*, or even a *piso*, according to the country where you are.

DEPARTMENT. En Estados Unidos, los *departments* son *ministerios*. (**Department of the Interior.** Ministerio del Interior.) Las tiendas con muchas secciones o *grandes tiendas* se llaman *department stores*.

DEPARTIR. *Departir* means *to chat, converse.* (**Departieron con mucho ingenio.** They had a witty chat.)

DEPART, DEPARTED. *To depart* es *partir, irse.* (**I will be ready to depart at any moment.** Estaré listo para salir en cualquier momento.) *Departed* puede ser un eufemismo por *fallecido*. (**The dear departed.** El querido finado.)

DEPENDENCIA. In an administrative setup, *dependencia* is a *unit,* a *branch,* normally lower than a department or a service. (**La Dependencia Común de Inspección practica estudios en la ONU.** The Joint Inspection Unit carries out surveys at the UN.)

DEPENDENCE. *Dependence* no plantea problemas especiales de traducción al español.

DEPENDIENTE. *Dependiente* is a worker in a subordinate position, for instance, *dependiente de tienda.* (**Sólo pudo obtener una plaza de dependiente de almacén.** He could only get a position as a warehouse employee.)

DEPENDABLE, DEPENDANT. *Dependable* es *fiable,* digno *de confianza.* (**As a treasurer, he is very dependable.** Como tesorero, es muy digno de confianza.) *Dependant* es quien depende de algo o alguien. (**The staff member gets an allowance for every dependant.** El funcionario obtiene una prestación por cada familiar a cargo.)

Depósito. A *depósito* is a *warehouse*. There are *depósitos judiciales* for vehicles involved in fatal accidents or simple breaches of the law, and *depósitos de cadáveres* or *morgues*.

Deposit. Muy específicamente, *deposit* puede querer decir *yacimiento* pero nunca *almacén*. (**Very rich oil deposits have been discovered in the country.** Se han descubierto en el país muy ricos yacimientos de petróleo.) En cuanto a ciertos depósitos específicos, *escrow* es un depósito en custodia, *bail* es una fianza o caución que debe presentar un inculpado, *trusteeship* un depósito confiado a un síndico que tiene la guarda de un menor o incapacitado, por lo general. Y, por cierto, *deposit* puede ser el *depósito de garantía* por un alquiler o venta inmobiliaria. *Security* es una voz muy utilizada para *depósito de garantía* o una garantía documental.

Derogar. *Derogar* means *to abolish, to repeal*. (**La vieja ley de inmigración se derogó a favor de una versión más restrictiva.** The old immigration law was repealed in favor of a more restrictive one.)

Derogate. *To derogate* quiere decir *detraer, menospreciar, denigrar*. (**With his comments, he derogated the majesty of the king.** Con sus comentarios denigró la majestad del rey.)

Desaprobar. *Desaprobar* is the opposite of *aprobar* (*to approve*). (**El Congreso desaprobó la política del ministro.** Congress did not approve the minister's policy.)

Disapprove, Disprove. Mientras *disapprove* es lo contrario de *approve*, *disprove* significa *refutar*. (**The father disapproved of the child's plans.** El padre no aprobó los proyectos del niño. **New findings disproved the theory.** Nuevos descubrimientos refutaron la teoría.)

DESCONTAR. There are various meanings of *descontar,* like cashing a letter of credit, or reducing a price by a certain discount, but it also has a surprising meaning: *to take for granted, to count on.* (**Descontó que María iria al baile.** She took it for granted that Maria would go to the dance.)

DISCOUNT. En inglés, *to discount* significa lo contrario de *descontar* en español: es *descartar, dejar de lado.* (**The manager discounted his opinion.** El gerente descartó su opinión.)

DESESPERADO. The Spanish word does not present translation problems.

DESPERATE, DESPERADO. *Desperate* se traduce normalmente por *desesperado.* (**She is desperate to please.** Está desesperada por saberse agradable.) *Desperado*, como lo saben los que ven películas del Lejano Oeste, es el *facineroso* perseguido por la justicia.

DESFILAR. No relation whatsoever to *defile. Desfilar* comes from *desfile* (*parade*). (**Desfilaron en formación de combate.** They paraded in combat formation.)

DEFILE. *To defile* es *deshonrar, profanar,* incluso *violar.* (**His comments defiled the memory of the deceased.** Sus comentarios mancillaron la memoria del finado.)

DESGRACIA, DESGRACIADO. The equivalent of *desgracia* is not *disgrace* but *misfortune.* (**Tuvo la desgracia de perder a su padre el mes pasado.** Last month he had the misfortune of losing his father.)

DISGRACE, DISGRACEFUL. En su acepción más común, *disgrace* no es simplemente *misfortune,* sino *ignominia, vergüenza, deshonra.* (**The court's acquittal of a confessed rapist is a disgrace.** La absolución por el tribunal de un violador confeso es una ignominia.)

DESINTERESADO. *Desinteresado* means *unselfish*, not *without interest*. (**Ayuda a su familia desinteresadamente.** He unselfishly helps his family.)

DISINTERESTED. Es *disinterested* el que ha perdido interés en algo. (**After his experience, he was disinterested in charitable work.** Después de su experiencia, perdió interés en las obras de caridad.) También *desinteresado* en el sentido de no tener un interés egoísta por algo. (**He gave a disinterested assistance to the poor couple.** Prestó una ayuda desinteresada a la pobre pareja.)

DESMAYO. *Desmayo* is translated by *fainting spell*. (**Al escuchar la noticia, se desmayó.** On hearing the news, he fainted.)

DISMAY. *Dismay* significa *consternación*. (**His words were received with dismay.** Sus palabras fueron recibidas con consternación.)

DESTITUCIÓN. *Destitución* is a noun derived from **destituir**: *to fire, dismiss, remove, downgrade*. (**El general fue destituido de sus funciones.** The general was stripped of his powers.)

DESTITUTION. *Destitution* es la *miseria abyecta*, el grado mayor de la pobreza. (**Civil war brought destitution to whole areas of the country.** Las guerras interiores provocaron una gran miseria en grandes regiones del país.)

DETERMINAR. *Determinar* is also used to mean *to verify*. (**El Cirujano Jefe ha determinado que fumar perjudica su salud.** The Surgeon General has determined that smoking is harmful to your health.)

DETERMINED. *To be determined* es *estar decidido a algo*. (**Determined to win the scholarship, he studied day and night.** Decidido a obtener la beca, estudió noche y día.)

DEVOLUCIÓN. In Spanish, this word comes from *devolver* (*to return*). (**No está permitida la devolución de ciertos artículos como bañadores.** The return of certain articles like swimsuits is not allowed.)

DEVOLUTION, DEVOLVE. *Devolution* es la *delegación de facultades*, de un gobierno central a una provincia, por ejemplo, que puede llegar a la *autonomía*. (**An aspiration of Northern Ireland nationalists was the devolution of government to the Irish citizenry.** Una aspiración de los independentistas de Irlanda del Norte era la cesión del gobierno a los ciudadanos irlandeses.) En la práctica de los negocios, puede traducirse por *decaer, degenerar*. (**What should have been a calm meeting devolved into bickering.** Lo que pudo ser una reunion tranquila degeneró en un intercambio de recriminaciones.)

DEVOTO. A person who is *devoto* actively follows the ideas and precepts of his religion. (**Es un católico devoto.** He is a devout Catholic.)

DEVOUT. Puede ser *devout,* no necesariamente de una religión, sino *consagrado, leal*. (**The manager is a devout worker.** El gerente es un trabajador consagrado a su tarea.)

DIGERIR, DIGESTO. The Spanish term *digerir* is always translated as *digest. Digesto* is the name given to an *official publication of the laws* and rules of a country or of one of its administrative units. (**El Digesto Municipal es útil para conocer las reglamentaciones urbanas al día.** The City Record is very useful if you want to be aware of the up-to-date urban regulations.)

DIGEST. Una versión abreviada de un libro o un artículo es un *digest*. (**Readers Digest is a successful magazine that carries abbreviated articles of general interest**. Selecciones del Readers Digest es una publicación exitosa con artículos abreviados de interés general.)

DIRECCIÓN. The most common meanings of *dirección* are *address, tendency, way.* (**Esta es mi dirección.** Here is my address.) It is then the equivalent of *señas.*

DIRECTIONS. En inglés, *directions* puede querer decir *instrucciones para llegar a algún lugar.* (**I will give you driving directions to get home.** Le daré instrucciones para llegar en coche a casa.)

DIRECTOR GENERAL, PRESIDENTE DE LA JUNTA DIRECTIVA, DIRECTOR EJECUTIVO (DELEGADO). *Presidente* is a position that can have different equivalents based on the staffing table of the body concerned. The **Presidente del Directorio** or **de la Junta Directiva** is the equivalent of *Chairman of the Board.* The **Director General** is equivalent to *President.*

PRESIDENT, CHAIRMAN OF THE BOARD, CHIEF EXECUTIVE OFFICER. A continuación se dan las equivalencias más comunes entre los dos idiomas. El **President** de una empresa es el *Director General,* mientras que **Chairman of the Board** es *el Presidente del Directorio o la Junta,* y el **Chief Executive Officer** el *Director Ejecutivo o Director Delegado.* En un cuerpo deliberativo, se llama **President** a quien ocupa esa dignidad por designación para un periodo prolongado, y **Chairman** o **Presiding Officer** por lo general para casos ocasionales o de breves períodos.

DIRECTORIO. A corporation is governed by its **Directorio** or **Junta de Directores.** (**En el Directorio había representantes de bancos y empresas de seguros.** The Board of Directors included representatives of banks and insurance companies.)

DIRECTORY. *Directory* es *un repertorio, un catálogo, un listín telefónico.* (**The hotel's directory of services was impressive.** La lista de servicios del hotel era abundante.)

DISCRECIÓN. *See* **Discreto.**

DISCRETO. The two words have similar meanings. *Discreto* may also mean *circumspect, inconspicuous.* (**Su discreta presencia pasaba inadvertida.** Because of his inconspicuous appearance he was barely noticeable.)

DISCREET. *Discreet* puede querer decir *mesurado, prudente, modesto* (el equivalente español de *modest* es *púdico, recatado*). Se emplea también mucho para calificar cifras o cantidades pequeñas. (**There was a discreet increase in the cost of living.** Hubo un modesto aumento en el costo de vida. **Richard had a discreet way of making his point.** Richard convencía de su idea de manera mesurada.)

DISCRIMINAR. Practically no difference in usage of both words.

DISCRIMINATE. *To discriminate* se emplea mucho en el sentido de *distinguir, diferenciar.* (**The wine specialist taught us to discriminate between a Bordeaux and a Bourgogne.** El experto en vinos nos enseñó a diferenciar un Burdeos de un Borgoña.)

DISCUTIR. *Discutir* often implies a *confrontation*, a challenge to another's position. (**Discutieron el precio de la carrera en el taxi.** They haggled over the price of the taxi ride.)

DISCUSS. En inglés, *to discuss* tiene un sentido neutral: significa *tratar, debatir.* (**The first point of the agenda was to discuss the world economic situation.** El primer punto del temario consistía en debatir la situación económica mundial.)

DISEMINAR. Spanish has just kept the original meaning: *to sow, spread, scatter.* (**El grano se diseminó en toda la propiedad.** The grain was sowed in the whole property.)

DISSEMINATE. La traducción normal de *to disseminate* es *difundir.* (**The news was disseminated everywhere.** La noticia se difundió por todas partes.)

DISGUSTANTE. *Disgustante* means simply *unpleasant.* (**Su conducta es disgustante.** His conduct is unpleasant.)

DISGUSTING. *Disgusting* es *desagradable*, y aún más, *repugnante.* (**To show those scenes on TV was disgusting.** Mostrar esas escenas por televisión era repugnante.)

DISGUSTO. In Spanish, *disgusto* means *annoyance, disagreement, sorrow, irritation, anger.* (**Sufrió un gran disgusto por la novedad.** The news irritated her.)

DISGUST. En inglés, esta palabra significa *falta de gusto* y quiere decir *aversión, repugnancia, hastío.* (**The public reacted with disgust to the crude language of the play.** El público reaccionó asqueado ante el lenguaje soez de la obra.)

DISIPAR. *Disipar* means *to evaporate, disappear.* (**La neblina se disipó a media mañana.** At mid-morning the mist dissipated.) But *disipar* also means *to squander.* (**Disipó su fortuna en malos negocios.** He squandered his fortune in bad business ventures.)

DISSIPATE. El participio *dissipated* puede traducirse como *disoluto, libertino.* (**He led a dissipated life.** Tenía una existencia disoluta.)

DISPARATE. A *disparate* is something *foolish, nonsense.* (**La obra es una colección de disparates.** The play is a series of foolish ideas.)

DISPARATE. El adjetivo *disparate* quiere decir *variado, dispar,* generalmente con un sentido negativo. (**The exhibit is a disparate series of works of art.** La exposición muestra una gran variedad de obras de arte.)

DISPENSAR, DISPENSA. *Dispensar* means *to pay* (attention), *to exempt someone from an obligation*, or *to confer a privilege*. (**Gracias por la atención dispensada.** Thank you for your attention.) A *dispensa* is an exemption granted by a church authority, an excuse or pardon. (**Dispensa de oir misa por enfermedad.** A dispensation to miss mass due to illness.)

DISPENSE. Hay varias acepciones de *to dispense* que recogen la idea de *repartir, distribuir* y que en español emplearían las palabras *administrar* (justicia), *preparar* (medicamentos), etc. (**A pharmacist dispenses drugs.** Un farmacéutico prepara medicamentos. **The family court dispenses justice in matters involving child guardianship.** El tribunal de familia administra justicia en cuestiones relativas a la guarda de los hijos.)

DISTRACCIÓN. *See* **Distraído.**

DISTRACTION.

DISTRAÍDO. *Distraído* is *absent-minded*. (**Cruzó distraído la calle sin advertir el coche que se acercaba.** He absentmindedly crossed the street without noticing the approaching car.)

DISTRACTED. *Distracted* quiere decir *aturdido, confundido, turbado*. (**He walked the streets distracted by the news.** Caminaba por las calles aturdido por la noticia.)

DIVERSIÓN. The Spanish term means *entertainment, amusement*. (**La diversión continuó hasta medianoche.** The merriment continued until midnight.)

DIVERSION. *Diversion* significa *desvío*. (**Road work on the highway made a diversion necessary.** Las obras de la carretera hicieron necesario el desvío.)

DIVERSO. *Diverso* means *distinct, different*. (**Diversos autores trataron el tema.** A variety of authors dealt with that topic.)

DIVERSE. *Variado* es el mejor equivalente de *diverse*. (**There was a diverse mixture of color in that modern painting.** El cuadro moderno tenía una variada mezcla de colores.)

DIVERTIR. (La concurrencia era muy divertida. The audience was quite amusing.)

See *Diversión* on previous page.

DIVERT. *To divert* es el verbo que corresponde al artículo anterior. **(A major accident forced the police to divert traffic from the highway to secondary roads.** Un gran accidente obligó a la policía a desviar el tráfico de la autopista hacia rutas secundarias.)

DIVISA. This Spanish word has different meanings that do not correspond to *device*: *foreign currency, emblem, motto.* **(La divisa europea aumentó un 5%.** European currency appreciated 5%. **En pueblos antiguos cada gremio exhibe su divisa en la puerta.** In old villages each profession displays its insignia on the door. **Vivir y dejar vivir es mi divisa.** To live and let live is my motto.)

DEVICE. *Device* quiere decir *artefacto, dispositivo, aparato.* **(The cell phone had a photographic device.** El teléfono celular tenía un dispositivo para sacar fotografías.) *To be left to his own devices* significa *dejar que resuelva un asunto por sí mismo.* **(The researcher left his assistant to his own devices.** El investigador dejó que su asistente se valiera por sí mismo.)

DIVORCIAR. No difference in usage between the Spanish and English terms.

DIVORCE. En un sentido figurado se utiliza este verbo con el significado de *desvincular.* **(You cannot understand the problem if you divorce causes from effects.** No comprenderás el problema si desvinculas los efectos de las causas.)

DOCTOR. No difference in usage between the Spanish and English terms.

DOCTOR. *To doctor* es *modificar algo al gusto de alguien.* **(He doctored the soup to make it more spicy.** Modificó la sopa para hacerla más picante.)

DOMESTICAR. *Domesticar* can be translated as *to tame*. (**En el circo, los leones no están del todo domesticados.** In the circus, lions are not completely tame.)

DOMESTICATE. La palabra *domesticate* suele usarse en un sentido figurado: *amansar, civilizar, hacer que una persona adopte hábitos domésticos*. (**A former guerrilla, he became domesticated.** Después de ser guerillero, se amansó.)

DOMÉSTICO. The English meaning has gained Spanish usage: *vuelos domésticos* (*domestic flights*), instead of *nacionales* or *de cabotaje*. (**Para combinar vuelos hay que pasar de la terminal internacional a la doméstica.** For connecting flights you have to transfer from the international to the domestic terminal.) A modern case of criminal conduct is that of *violencia doméstica*, sometimes referred to as *violencia de género*. See **Género**.

DOMESTIC. Hoy se dice *vuelos domésticos* por intrusión del inglés, en lugar de *vuelos nacionales, de cabotaje*. Tal vez pronto se diga *producto bruto doméstico* para hablar del *producto interior bruto*.

DORMITORIO. *Dormitorio* is *bedroom* in English. (**En América Latina el dormitorio se conoce también como alcoba o recámara.** In Latin America, the bedroom is called *dormitorio, alcoba* or *recámara*.)

DORMITORY. *Dormitory* se aplica a una *residencia universitaria*, no a un simple lugar para dormir. (**She was excited to go to college and live in the dormitory, despite having to share a tiny room with a stranger.** Estaba entusiasmada por ir a la Universidad y vivir en la residencia, a pesar de tener que compartir una habitación pequeña con una extraña.)

DRAMÁTICO. Derived from *drama*, this term has no secondary meaning. (**Tuvo una existencia dramática.** Her life was a drama.)

DRAMATIC. El adjetivo *dramatic* se usa como expresión gráfica para denotar algo *espectacular, extraordinario, grandioso.* (**Life expectancy had a dramatic increase in the last two decades.** Ha habido un aumento espectacular de la esperanza de vida en los últimos veinte años.)

DUELO. *Duelo* is normally translated as *duel.* It may also mean grieving after someone's death, and then it is rendered as *bereavement, mourning.* (**La bandera nacional fue izada a media asta en señal de duelo por el difunto presidente.** The flag was at half mast in a show of mourning for the deceased president.)

DUEL. *El combate a la antigua entre dos enemigos* se expresa con la palabra *duel.*

ECONOMÍA. *Economía* may indicate a *limitation of the means* assigned to a certain purpose. (**Con economía de esfuerzo logró poner en marcha el coche.** With little effort he succeeded in starting the car.)

ECONOMICS, ECONOMY. *Economics* alude a la *ciencia de la economía.* (**He graduated in economics.** Se graduó en ciencias económicas.) *The economy* es una manera abreviada de aludir a la *situación económica.* (**The national economy is at a good juncture.** La situación económica nacional pasa por un buen momento.)

EDIFICACIÓN. The meaning of the Spanish word is *construction, build-up, building.* (**La edificación en el centro es muy compacta.** Construction downtown is quite dense.)

EDIFICATION. Hacer algo *for the edification of someone* es hacerlo para su ilustración, para su gobierno. (**The researching doctor gave a briefing for the edification of the participants.** El médico investigador dio una charla informativa para ilustración de los participantes.)

EDIFICAR. *Edificar* means *to build.* (**En España, la ley de costas prohíbe edificar a menos de 500 metros del mar.** In Spain, the law regulating the seashore forbids building within 500 yards of the sea.)

EDIFY. Se usa *edify* cuando se *ilustra, educa o aclara algo* o cuando se predica con el ejemplo. (**His edifying conduct inspired the students.** Su comportamiento edificante inspiró a los estudiantes.)

EDITAR. In Spanish *editar* is *to publish.* (**Una casa prestigiosa editó su libro.** A prestigious firm published his book.)

EDIT. *To edit* es *hacer una revisión,* por lo general de estilo y cotejo con las fuentes, aunque puede ir más a fondo en la comprobación del material. (**Several translators worked on the book, making it necessary to edit the draft.** Varios traductores trabajaron en el libro, lo que hizo necesario una revisión a fondo del borrador.)

EDITOR. An *editor* in Spanish is whoever *publishes* (*edita*) a book. (**Muchos editores realizan concursos anuales buscando nuevos autores.** Many publishers hold annual competitions in search of new authors.)

EDITOR. En un periódico o revista, el *editor,* a diferencia del *publisher* (*director*), es el *secretario (o jefe) de redacción.* (**At major papers, the editor maintains independence from the publisher.** En los grandes periódicos, el jefe de redacción mantiene su independencia del director.)

EDITORIAL. An *editorial* is a *publishing house*. Here is another word that has yielded to the English influence: what used to be called an **artículo de fondo** (*main editorial statement*) is now also called **editorial** (or **artículo editorial**).

EDITORIAL. (**The editorial is a statement of policy of the paper on a major question.** El artículo de fondo es una declaración de política del periódico sobre un tema importante.)

EDUCADO. In Spanish, *educado* can mean *cultured* or *well mannered*. (**Es un joven muy educado.** He is a cultured young man. **Sus hijos son muchachos bien educados.** He has children with good manners.)

EDUCATED. *Educated* en su sentido original se refiere a la preparación escolar, pero ambién tiene un sentido figurado.

EGREGIO. These words have quite different meanings: *egregio,* faithful to its Latin origin, means *illustrious, distinguished.* (**Lo operó un egregio cirujano.** He was operated on by a famous surgeon.)

EGREGIOUS. En inglés, la palabra ha evolucionado hacia una connotación negativa: *tremendo, atroz, exageradamente tonto, estúpido.* (**His ignorance is egregious.** Es de una ignorancia supina.)

EJECUTANTE, EJECUTAR, EJECUTOR. *Ejecutante* is *player, executant,* while *ejecutor* is the *executor* of a will. (**Designó a su sobrina ejecutora testamentaria.** He named his niece the executor of his will.)

EXECUTANT, EXECUTIONER, EXECUTOR. Solía decir en broma que un mal pianista *ejecutaba* a Chopin. Pues bien, **executioner** no es el *ejecutante* sino el *verdugo.* (**The executioner waited at the foot of the scaffold.** El verdugo esperaba al pie del patíbulo. **The executant made his debut at Carnegie Hall.** El ejecutante hacía su debut en el Carnegie Hall.)

ELABORAR. The normal meaning of *elaborar* is *to manufacture*, with the idea of some complexity. (**Producto elaborado en Francia para el público de los Estados Unidos.** Made in France for American consumption.)

ELABORATE. En ingles, *to elaborate* significa *detallar, explayarse, hacer algo minucioso o complejo.* (**The delegate elaborated on his proposal.** El delegado se explayó sobre su propuesta.)

ELOGIAR. *Elogiar* is *to extol, to praise*. (**Se elogió su gusto en la elección del mobiliario.** There was praise for his taste in the choice of the furniture.)

EULOGIZE. *To eulogize* es *pronunciar una oración de recordación* y homenaje a un desaparecido. (**The qualities of the deceased were eulogized.** Fueron encomiadas las virtudes del finado.)

ELOGIO. There can be *elogio* of a living person, not necessarily a *eulogy*. (**El autor del sermón se ganó el elogio.** The author of the sermon deserved praise.)

EULOGY. *Eulogy* se utiliza sobre todo para una *oración fúnebre.* (**The priest gave a moving eulogy.** El sacerdote pronunció una conmovedora oración fúnebre.)

EMBARAZAR. *Embarazar* is *to make pregnant*. (**Estaba embarazada desde hacía cuatro meses.** She was four months pregnant.)

EMBARRASS. Muy distinto es el sentido de *to embarrass*: *poner en aprietos*, en situación desmañada, *avergonzar*. (**He admitted, embarrassed, that he made the mistake.** Admitió avergonzado que había cometido el error.)

EMBARGO. No particular Spanish deviation from the English word.

EMBARGO. Fuera de las acepciones comunes de esta palabra, se dice de un documento que no está listo para ser difundido que está bajo *embargo*. (**The advance copy of the speech was embargoed until delivered.** No podía difundirse el ejemplar anticipado del discurso hasta haber sido pronunciado.)

ENDEUDADO. To be *endeudado* is *to have debts*, generally of importance. (**Los países muy endeudados lograron el alivio de su deuda.** The heavily indebted countries benefited from debt relief.)

INDEBTED. Una persona puede estar *indebted* con otra por un favor recibido. (**He was indebted to his mentor for his advice on the development of his career.** Se hallaba en deuda con su mentor por sus consejos sobre la evolución de su carrera.)

ENDOSAR. In Spanish, *endosar* is *to transmit a commercial instrument.* (**Endosó a su mujer el cheque del seguro.** He endorsed the insurance check over to his wife.)

ENDORSE. *Endorse* significa *trasmitir un documento comercial.* Además, en términos parlamentarios, *to endorse* significa *hacer suya, apoyar, secundar* una moción o propuesta. (**Most countries endorsed the proposal to make Arabic an official language.** La mayoría de los países apoyó la propuesta de hacer del árabe una lengua oficial.)

ENFERMEDAD. *Sickness, illness* and *disease* are equivalents of *enfermedad.* (**Enfermedades contagiosas.** Communicable diseases.)

INFIRMITY. Con *infirmity* se designa un *defecto físico, una tara* o *minusvalía.* (**His infirmity was such that he could not walk.** Estaba tan achacoso que no podía caminar.)

ENFERMO. *Enfermo* is *ill, sick.* (**Está enfermo de cuidado.** He is very sick.)

INFIRM. *Infirm* puede ser *achacoso, débil* o con algún defecto serio, *tullido.* (**The infirm get special care.** Se presta atención especial a los muy débiles.)

ENORMIDAD. *Enormidad* is normally applied to the *enormous* size of something. **(La enormidad del camión atemoriza.** The tremendous size of the truck is frightening.)

ENORMITY. Si bien *enormity* suele ser una descripción de la magnitud de una cosa, suele usarse como *atrocidad, monstruosidad.* **(One cannot deny the enormity of the crimes committed under the Third Reich.** No se puede negar la monstruosidad de los crímenes cometidos durante el Third Reich.)

ENSAYO. Apart from the common meaning of *test, ensayo* means *rehearsal.* **(Varios ensayos precedieron al concierto.** There were several rehearsals before the concert. **Nuevos medicamentos se ensayan en ratas.** New medicines are tested on rats.)

ESSAY. Se usa *essay* para un *suelto periodistico* o una *composición escolar.* **(The Op-Ed page of the *Times* publishes essays by distinguished journalists.** En la página frente al artículo de fondo del *Times* se publican sueltos de periodistas distinguidos.)

ENTRADA. *Entrada* is *entry* or *way in.* **(Un cartel prohíbe la entrada a esa habitación.** There is a "no entry" sign to that room.)

ENTRY. El significado original de *entry* or *way in* es *entrada.* En una lista, diccionario, enciclopedia, es preferible traducir *entry* por *artículo,* aunque el DRAE ya recoge la acepción de *entrada* para el caso. En términos contables, *entry* se traduce por *asiento* o *partida.* **(Bookkeeping there is done with the double entry system.** Allí la contabilidad se lleva con el sistema de partida doble. **For each transaction there is an entry.** Hay un asiento por transacción.)

ENTRAR. *Entrar* is more usual than *enter* in daily speech. To allow entry, it is common to say *¡Adelante!*

ENTER. *Enter* suena más culterano que *come in*. Una traducción más apropiada, según el caso, puede ser *ingresar, incorporar, rellenar*. (**A new character enters the scene.** Un nuevo personaje ingresa al escenario.)

ENTRETENER. *Entretener* means *to amuse*. (**Fue una velada entretenida.** It was an amusing evening.)

ENTERTAIN. El uso más frecuente de *to entertain* es *recibir* en el sentido de *agasajar, ser anfitrión*. (**To entertain requires taste, diplomacy and a good dose of food and drink.** Para recibir, hace falta gusto, diplomacia y una buena dosis de comida y bebida.)

ENTRETENIMIENTO. *Entretenimiento* is a *pastime*. (**Pasaba su tiempo con entretenimientos en lugar de estudiar seriamente.** Instead of being engaged in serious studies, he frittered away his time.)

ENTERTAINMENT. En una fiesta los artistas proporcionan *entertainment*. (**That evening, the entertainment was provided by a musical combo.** Amenizaba la velada un conjunto musical.)

ENVIDIOSO. To be *envidioso* is to be *jealous* or *envious*. (**Sufría por envidioso al ver avanzar a su hermano.** Envy for his brother's progress had him suffering.)

INVIDIOUS. *Invidious* es *denigrante, ofensivo* y, por lo tanto, *injusto*. (**It was an invidious comparison.** Fue una comparación ofensiva.)

ENVOLVER, INVOLUCRAR. *Envolver* is *to wrap* or *to pack*. (**Envuélvalo con una cinta.** Wrap it with a ribbon.)

INVOLVE. Un asunto puede *involve*, o *involucrar* distintos elementos, o a personas o cosas. (**The whole village was involved in the preparation of the welcoming party for the winner of the prize.** Todo el pueblo participó en los preparativos de la fiesta de bienvenida al galardonado. **The statement involves all the fundamental human rights.** En la declaración están involucrados todos los derechos humanos fundamentales.)

EQUIDAD. Terms equivalent to *equidad* are *fairness, impartiality*. (**La equidad es la base de las buenas relaciones laborales.** Fairness is the basis of good relations in the workplace.)

EQUITY. *Equity* es el *capital accionario*. (**The buying company paid half of the price with equity.** La compañía adquirente pagó la mitad del precio en capital accionario.)

EQUIVOCAR. *Equivocar(se)* is *to make a mistake*. (**Se equivocó de tren rápido.** He mistook an express train for another.)

EQUIVOCATE. La palabra inglesa no significa *equivocarse* sino *engañar mediante un lenguaje equívoco, de doble sentido, insincero o tratar de disfrazar la intención.* (**Equivocating, he avoided making a decision.** Con artimañas, trató de evitar decidirse.)

ERRANTE. Derived from *errar*, *errante* means *wandering*. (**El holandés errante.** The wandering Dutchman.)

ERRAND. *Errand* es un *mandado*, una *diligencia*. (**When you called, I was running errands.** Cuando llamaste, había salido a hacer unas diligencias.)

ERRAR. *Errar* means *to make a mistake*, but has another sense: *wander*. (**De noche erró sin rumbo.** He wandered that night with no direction.)

ERR. *To err on the side of caution* significa *ser impreciso o erróneo por cautela*. Por extensión de la acepción de *vagar*, se entiende por esta palabra *descarriarse*. (**He erred in his calculations.** Erró en sus calculos.)

ESCALA. *Escala* means *range*, or otherwise *ladder*. (**Los profesores califican en una escala de 1 a 10.** Teachers give grades in a range from 1 to 10. **Sostén la escala.** Hold the ladder.)

SCALE. *Scale* significa también *balanza* o *báscula*. (**On some roads trucks are required to be weighed on the municipal scale before driving through a village.** En algunas carreteras se exige a los camiones el peso en la báscula municipal antes de atravesar el pueblo.)

ESCAPE. *Escape* is the *exhaust* of a car. (**Por el escape salen gases tóxicos.** Noxious gases escape in the exhaust.)

ESCAPE. En español pueden corresponder a *to escape* toda una serie de palabras relacionadas semánticamente pero que requieren precisión, como *evadir*, *huir*, *olvidarse*, *etc*. (**He escaped the tax man by operating in a financial haven.** Evadió la tributación trabajando en un refugio financiero. **He escaped punishment after a false testimony.** Evitó el castigo por un falso testimonio. **An escape from reality.** Una evasión de la realidad.)

Escasamente. *Escasamente* means *almost*, *barely*. (**Había recorrido escasamente cien metros cuando tuvo el accidente.** He had barely gone one hundred yards when he had the accident.)

Scarcely. Al decir *scarcely* se duda de que algo pueda ocurrir. La probabilidad no es escasa sino prácticamente nula. (**He would run scarcely two miles of the marathon.** Apenas si correría dos millas de la maratón.)

Escenario. *Escenario o escena* is *the stage*, the part of the theater where a play or a concert is performed. (**Para el concierto del pianista se habían dispuesto asientos en el escenario.** Seats were arranged on the stage for the piano concert.)

Scenario. *Scenario* quiere decir *guión*, *argumento*, y también *hipótesis*, *premisa*, y con este sentido se utiliza mucho en presentaciones políticas o académicas. (**They worked on the scenario for a new film.** Trabajaron en el guión de una nueva película. **This scenario implies a policy of open markets.** Esta hipótesis se basa en la situación de mercados abiertos.) Cuando se habla del *worst possible scenario*, se quiere decir *la peor situación posible, la hipótesis menos favorable*.

Escolar. *Escolar* is a *student*, normally of the first cycle. (**Los escolares prestaban atención al maestro.** The pupils paid attention to the teacher.)

Scholar. En el otro extremo de la gama que empieza con escolar está precisamente el *scholar*, el *académico* y, por extensión, un *erudito* en determinada materia. (**He is the most famous scholar of Middle Eastern affairs.** Es el más erudito en asuntos del Oriente Medio.)

ESLORA. This is a marine term that has no English equivalent; it is defined as *the length of a boat*. (**Tenía un magnífico barco de 40 metros de eslora.** He had a magnificent boat 40 meters long.)

ESPECTÁCULO. *Espectáculo* can be translated as *spectacle* or *show*. (**Un espectáculo terrible: la película de atrocidades policiales contra minorías.** An awful spectacle: the filmed police atrocities against minorities. **El espectáculo de TV obtuvo una crítica excelente.** The TV show had a great review.)

SPECTACLES. *Spectacles* o *glasses* son los que en España y América Latina reciben también nombres diferentes, como *gafas*, *lentes*, *anteojos*, *espejuelos*. (**I wear these prescription spectacles all the time.** Uso permanentemente estas gafas recetadas.)

ESPÍRITU. The original meanings are the same in English and Spanish.

SPIRIT. *Spirit* puede ser una *bebida alcohólica*, lo que en español también se traduce por *bebida espirituosa*. Recuerda aquella historia de la máquina de traducir, que para **The flesh is weak but the spirit is strong** (La carne es débil, pero el espíritu es fuerte) dio **La carne está podrida, pero el alcohol es mucho.**

ESPIRITUALISTA. Both words refer to the follower of a philosophical school, spiritualism. But the Spanish usage makes it a synonym of *idealista*. (**Es espiritualista en extremo.** He is an extreme idealist.)

SPIRITUALIST. El uso inglés suele convertir *espiritualista* en *espiritista*. (**My friend goes to meetings of a spiritualist group.** Mi amigo asiste a una reunión de un grupo espiritista.)

ESTACIONARIO. *Estacionario* is used as an adjective to describe satellites that have a geosynchronous orbit. (**La television por satélite utiliza la órbita estacionaria.** Satellite TV uses a stationary orbit.)

STATIONARY, STATIONERY. *Stationary* quiere decir *inmóvil*, que no avanza ni retrocede. (**The caravan remained stationary.** La caravana permaneció inmóvil.) *Stationery* son los *útiles y papeles de escritorio* y, por extensión, se llama así a las *librerías* o *papelerías*. (**You may find all sorts of papers at the stationer's.** Encontrarás papel de todas clases en la papelería.)

ESTAMPA. *Estampa* is an *image* or a *religious print* or *engraving*. The word *estampilla*, used mostly in Latin America, as well as the Spanish *sello*, is translated as *stamp*. (**La monja le regaló una estampa de la Virgen.** The nun gave her a picture of the Virgin.)

STAMP. Múltiples significados tiene la palabra *stamp*: *sello, estampilla, timbre, molde, grabado*. (**Many government forms require the use of a fee stamp.** Hay que colocar un timbre con el importe de la tasa en muchos papeles oficiales.)

ESTANCIA. *Estancia* is a *room*, or in general *living quarters*, and also the *duration of a stay in a place*. (**Su estancia en el hospital se prolongó cinco días.** His stay in the hospital was extended for five days. **La casa tenía una amplia estancia frente al mar.** The house had a big room facing the sea.) In Argentina particularly, *estancia* is a large country estate with living quarters and a huge complex for cattle and crops, like a *ranch* in the United States.

ESTATE. *Estate* es el *patrimonio*, particularmente de una herencia. (**The estate of the deceased included many houses in choice locations.** El caudal hereditario incluía muchas casas en lugares de excepción.) *Real estate* es la *propiedad inmobiliaria* o *bienes raíces*. (**The value of real estate in New York has increased threefold in the last ten years.** El valor de la propiedad inmobiliaria se ha triplicado en Nueva York en el último decenio.)

ESTIMA, ESTIMACIÓN, ESTIMAR. *Estimación* o *estima* means *esteem*, a synonym of *aprecio*. (**Le tengo en gran estima por su generosidad.** I have great esteem for him as a generous person.)

ESTIMATE, ESTEEM. Un *estimate* es un *cálculo*, un *presupuesto*, algo más concreto que una estimación. (**Repair shops are supposed to give you an estimate of the repairs to be made on your car.** Los talleres están obligados a proporcionarle un presupuesto de las reparaciones que harán a su coche.) También se emplea para *juzgar*, *evaluar*. (**The expert estimated the value of the picture.** El experto juzgó el valor del cuadro.) No se usa el verbo por *tener estima* o *consideración*.

EVENTO. The Spanish Royal Academy has accepted *evento* as *special occasion, occurrence*, a regionalism in certain Latin American countries.

EVENT. *In the event of* es *en caso de, en la eventualidad de que*. (**Do not use elevators in the event of fire.** No utilice los ascensores en caso de incendio.)

EVENTUAL(MENTE). *Eventual* applies to a thing that may or may not happen. (**Un suceso eventual puede cambiar la suerte de un negocio.** An unforeseen event can change the fortunes of a business venture.) *Trabajador eventual* refers to a *temporary*, often *seasonal* *worker*. In a budget context, *gastos eventuales* o *imprevistos* applies to *unforeseen expenses*.

EVENTUAL(LY). En inglés, *eventual* conlleva la idea de finalidad, de *destino último*, pero en español se trata de algo *imprevisto* o *sujeto a contingencia*. (**Eventually, all buses will be equipped to transport handicapped people.** En definitiva, todos los autobuses estarán equipados para trasladar a minusválidos.)

EVIDENCIA. In Spanish *evidencia* is *certitude*, something that cannot be discussed. (**Probado hasta la evidencia.** It has been proved conclusively.)

EVIDENCE. *Evidence* es el término jurídico que describe un *elemento de prueba*, con un substrato más o menos neutral. (**The prosecution presented many pieces of evidence.** El fiscal presentó muchos elementos de prueba.)

EXACTO. *Exacto* is *accurate*, *right*. (**La cifra exacta es mil.** One thousand is the correct figure.)

EXACT. El verbo *to exact* significa *exigir*. (**The nationalist Basques exacted a support "tax" from local businessmen.** Los nacionalistas vascos exigían un "ïmpuesto" de apoyo a los empresarios locales.)

EXALTAR. *Exaltar* is *to praise*, *to extol*, *glorify*. (**Exaltó la figura del héroe con un elocuente discurso.** He praised the hero's character in an eloquent speech.)

EXALT. Entre los significados de *to exalt* están *elevar la jerarquía, el poder o el carácter*, e *inspirar, estimular*. (**The countryside exalted the composer's imagination.** La campiña inspiró la imaginación del compositor.)

EXCEPCIÓN. In both languages, the meaning is *something that escapes the general rule*.

EXCEPTION, EXEMPTION. *To take exception* es *objetar, rechazar*. (**The Israeli delegate took exception to the statement of the Arab League.** El delegado israelí rechazó la declaración de la Liga Árabe.) En una declaración del impuesto a la renta las deducciones son *exemptions*. (**The accountant listed all the allowed exemptions.** El contable enumeró todas las deducciones permitidas.)

EXCEPTUABLE. *Exceptuable* means that it should be excluded. (**Hay partidas exceptuables del impuesto a la renta.** There are items than can be deducted for income taxes.)

EXCEPTIONABLE. *Exceptionable* quiere decir *objetable, impugnable, recusable.* (**His behavior was exceptionable, improper of a friend.** Su conducta fue objetable, impropia de un amigo.)

EXCITANTE. *Excitante* may be best rendered by *stimulant* (not *exciting*). (**La cafeína es un excitante.** Caffeine is a stimulant.)

EXCITING. Como adjetivo, *exciting* se aplicaría también a lo dicho en el artículo anterior. (***Exciting news about your progress.*** Una noticia entusiasmante sobre sus progresos.)

EXCITAR. The meaning of *excitar* is normally confined to the physical result of *nervousness, agitation.* (**Regresó excitado por tantos trámites.** He returned agitated after so much bureaucracy.)

EXCITE. Es mejor traducir *to excite* por *estimular, acicatear.* (**The travel guide excited the appetite for a tour of Asia.** La guía de viajes estimuló el deseo de una gira por Asia.)

ÉXITO. The happy conclusion of a business deal or a performance is called *éxito.* (**Sus negociaciones se vieron coronadas por un rotundo éxito.** His negotiations ended in a resounding success.)

EXIT. *Exit* en inglés es *salida.* (**Take exit 38 for the museum.** Toma la salida 38 para llegar al museo.)

EXPEDIENTE. *Expediente* is a *file.* (**Se trata de un expediente muy complejo, que llena muchas páginas.** It is a very complex file comprising many pages.)

EXPEDIENT. *Expedient* quiere decir *oportuno, ventajoso, apropiado.* (**The judge is looking for an expedient resolution of the case.** El juez procura resolver el caso adecuadamente.)

EXPLICAR. The simple translation of *explicar* is *to explain*. (**Me explicaron su opinión.** His view was explained to me.)

EXPLICATE. El contenido semántico de *explicate* es más amplio que *explicar*, aunque sean de la misma etimología. En el primer caso se trata de *exponer en detalle, desarrollar*. (**You will have to explicate the ins and outs of the matter.** Tendrás que detallar todos los aspectos de la cuestión.)

EXPLOTAR. *Explotar* is translated as *to explode*. (**El grupo terrorista hizo explotar un artefacto en el mercado.** The terrorist group exploded a device in the market.)

EXPLOIT. Como sustantivo, *exploit* significa *hazaña, proeza*. El verbo *to exploit* significa *aprovecharse de algo* y también *promover, despertar interés*. (**Climbing Everest is a great exploit.** Ascender al Everest es una gran hazaña. **The boxer exploited his opponent's weaknesses.** El boxeador explotó las delibidades de su contrincante.)

EXPONER. In Spanish *exponer* means *to expound* and also *to show, to exhibit*. (**El autor expuso la idea que informa su obra.** The writer expounded on the idea behind his work. **El artista expuso en una gran galería.** The artist had an exhibit in an important gallery.)

EXPOSE. Una acepción común de *to expose* es *revelar, hacer público, desenmascarar*. (**The revelations exposed him to the public.** Las revelaciones lo desenmascararon ante el público.)

EXTENDER. The Spanish and Englsih words have analogous meanings.

EXTEND. Aparte de los significados comunes a las dos voces, *to extend* puede significar *ofrecer*, *dirigir* como en el caso de una invitación. (**The former enemy extended his hand to him in sign of reconciliation.** El antiguo enemigo le ofreció la mano como prenda de reconciliación.)

EXTENSIÓN. As in *size, expanse*, etc., these words have meanings common to both languages.

EXTENT, EXTENSION. *Extent* es *un límite*, un punto hasta el cual se mide y considera algo. (**I can operate computers up to a certain extent.** Sé utilizar ordenadores hasta cierto punto. **The extent of my knowledge is quite limited.** Mis conocimientos son muy limitados.) Las universidades dictan también *extension courses*, dirigidos al público en general. (**New York University has many extension programs.** La Universidad de Nueva York tiene muchos programas de divulgación.)

EXTENUAR. *Extenuar* is a synonym of *debilitar, agotar* (*weaken, exhaust*). (**La marcha lo dejó extenuado.** The walk left him exhausted.)

EXTENUATE. *To extenuate* significa *mitigar, paliar*. (**The counsel for the defense adduced extenuating circumstances for the crime.** El abogado defensor adujo circunstancias atenuantes del delito.)

EXTORSIÓN. *Extorsión* is the Spanish word for the Gallicism *chantage*. (**Los separatistas practican la extorsión con los comerciantes.** The separatists practice extortion on businessmen.)

EXTORTION. Además del sentido habitual de *chantaje*, puede denotar la idea más general de *exacción*. (**The official guilty of extortion was suspended.** Fue suspendido el funcionario culpable de exacción.)

EXTRAÑAR. *Extrañar* may mean *to miss* or *to surprise*. (**Extrañarán al antiguo director.** The old conductor will be missed. **Extrañó la actitud del público.** The audience reaction was a surprise.)

ESTRANGE. La voz inglesa se traduce por *separar(se)*, *enajenar*. (**The estranged couple have no relationship.** Los cónyuges separados no mantienen relaciones.)

EXTRANJERO, EXTRAÑO. *Extranjero* means *foreign*, *alien* being used officially in immigration proceedings, or in modern science fiction to designate a *space creature* (also *alienígena*); *extraño* is *rare* or *stranger*. (**Un extranjero sin residencia en el país.** A non-resident alien. **Se sentía como un extraño en la ciudad.** He felt like a stranger in the city.)

FOREIGNER, STRANGER. Es materia de uso, hay varias palabras (*stranger*, *alien*, *foreign*) que contienen la misma idea: *strange* es *lo poco común, raro, fuera de lugar*; *alien lo distinto, ajeno*; *foreign* o *stranger* el *extranjero* o *forastero*. (**A stranger in these places.** Un extraño en este sitio. **Coffee is alien to the Japanese.** El café es ajeno a los japoneses. **To learn a foreign language is to widen one's horizons.** Aprender un idioma extranjero es ampliar tus miras.)

EXTRAVAGANTE. In Spanish, *extravagante* is something or someone *unusual, out of the ordinary*. (**Las modelos me parecen siempre que visten ropa fea y extravagante en los desfiles de modas.** To me, models in fashion shows look like they wear awful, very unusual dresses.)

EXTRAVAGANT. *Extravagant* tiene en inglés el sentido de *despilfarro, falta de moderación, disparate*. (**In spite of his modest means, he spends extravagantly on clothes.** A pesar de sus medios de fortuna limitados, acostumbra derrochar en ropa.)

FÁBRICA. *Fábrica* means *factory, manufacturer*. (**En Estados Unidos hay más fábricas japonesas de automóviles que americanas.** In the United States there are more Japanese car manufacturers than American ones.)

FABRIC. *Fabric* es una *tela*, la *trama* de un tejido, y por extensión el *meollo*, la característica singular de algo. (**The very fabric of his political theory is faulty.** El meollo de su teoría política es defectuoso.)

FABRICAR, FABRICACIÓN. *Fabricar* is *to manufacture*, and *fabricación*, the *manufacture of*. (**La fabricación del papel se come anualmente millones de árboles.** The manufacture of paper eats up millions of trees annually.)

FABRICATE, FABRICATION. En un sentido figurado, pero bastante usual, *to fabricate* significa *falsificar, inventar, manipular algo*. (**He fabricated an excuse to absent himself.** Inventó una excusa para ausentarse.)

FACILIDAD. *Facilidad* is the quality of being *fácil, easy*. (**Facilidades de pago.** Easy terms. **Fácil de usar.** User friendly.)

FACILITY. *Facility* no significa necesariamente *facilidad* sino *instalación, servicio*. (**A new facility of the World Bank deals wih the debt relief.** Un nuevo servicio del Banco Mundial se ocupa del alivio de la deuda.)

FACTORÍA. *Factoría* evokes an industrial establishment in a colonial country. (**Las factorías coloniales empleaban en condiciones de esclavitud.** Colonial factories employed workers in slave-like conditions.)

FACTORY. El término usual para una manufactura es *factory*. (**The old factory is now a museum.** La antigua factoría es hoy un museo.)

FACULTAD. Among the different meanings of *facultad* there is *authority* or *capacity* and also the specialized department or school of a university. (**El tesorero tiene la facultad de firmar cheques para caja chica.** The treasurer has authority to sign checks for petty cash. **La Facultad de Derecho ofrece varias carreras.** The School of Law offers different careers.)

FACULTY. *Faculty*, además de aptitud, tiene el significado específico de *cuerpo docente*. (**The faculty included well-known researchers.** En el cuerpo docente había investigadores conocidos.)

FACULTATIVO. Apart from the common meaning of both words, *facultativo* is another name for a *physician* or *doctor*. (**El facultativo prescribió reposo.** The doctor ordered rest.)

FACULTATIVE. *Facultative*, en un sentido usado con poca frecuencia, es el equivalente de *facultativo* en su sentido de *opcional*. (**That subject was facultative.** Esa materia era de enseñanza facultativa.)

FALACIA. In Spanish, *falacia* is a *fraud*, *something false*, *designed to disorient*. (**Confundir nobleza con sabiduría es una falacia.** It is a gross mistake to confuse nobility with wisdom.)

FALLACY. En inglés, *fallacy* quiere decir tan sólo *error*. (**To think of him as a rich man is a fallacy.** Es un error creer que es rico.)

FALLA, FALLO, FALTA. *Falla* (in Spain, more generally *fallo*) is a *defect*, a *breakdown*. (**El coche se detuvo por un fallo en el carburador.** The car broke down because of a defect in the carburetor.) But *fallo* is also *sentence*, *decision*. (**El fallo del tribunal favoreció al demandante.** The court's sentence was in favor of the plaintiff.)

FAULT. Tanto para *fallo* (*avería, error*) como para *falta* y *falla geológica* se utiliza *fault*. (**Some countries have established a no-fault divorce.** Hay países que han instituido el divorcio sin declaración de falta de parte. **The fault spanning the west of the Americas is responsible for many earthquakes.** La falla geológica que recorre el oeste de las Américas ha provocado muchos terremotos. **A fault is the lowest grade of breaches of the law.** Una falta es la categoría inferior de contravenciones legales. **I found fault with your argument.** Encontré un fallo en su argumentación.)

FASTIDIOSO. In Spanish, *fastidioso* is *annoying, bothersome*. (**A fuerza de estar siempre preguntando, resulta fastidioso.** He is a bother, always asking questions.)

FASTIDIOUS. Hay aquí una divergencia semántica interesante. En inglés, *fastidious* pasó de molesto o importuno a *quisquilloso, minucioso, melindroso*. (**The chef fastidiously checked every ingredient.** El jefe de cocina examinaba minuciosamene todos los ingredients.)

FATIGA. *Fatiga* is *tiredness.* **(La fatiga injustificada puede ser signo de un problema cardíaco.** Undue tiredness may point to a heart condition.)

FATIGUE. En términos militares, *fatigue* es normalmente un adjetivo que quiere decir *de fajina* o *faena, de campaña. Fatigues* puede traducirse también como *ropa de entrecasa.* **(Soldiers were training in fatigues.** Los soldados se entrenaban en ropa de fajina.) *Metal fatigue* es la fatiga del material, principalmente de los aviones, que hace algunas décadas se descubrió como causante de varias catástrofes.

FECHAS, HORAS. Differences in usage can confuse the translator. In the Spanish-Latin American usage, dates are given in the order day-month-year, more rarely year-month-day. Hours are in the 24-hour cycle, the way they are used in the U.S. Armed Forces, for instance. In the popular usage, though, it is common to speak of *las 10 de la mañana o las 10 de la noche* (strictly, 22 hours).

DATES, TIME. Hay usos diferentes en la notación de fechas y horas. En los Estados Unidos, se dan las fechas en el orden mes-día-año, más raramente año-mes-día. En los Estados Unidos y algunos países cercanos se indica *a.m.* (ante meridiano) para la mañana y *p.m.* (post meridiano) para la tarde. Las 12 del mediodía se designa como *12 noon*, aunque también se usa *12 pm* (un absurdo lógico ya que *m* designa el meridiano del mediodía), y a las 12 de medianoche suele aludirse como *12 am*. La primera hora de la mañana, el comienzo del día, va de las 12 (no 0 hora) a 1, y se cuenta como 12 y minutos. Es común ver en horarios del transporte la mención de 11.59 y 12.01 para evitar confusiones en las cercanías de las 12.

FELONÍA. In Spanish, *felonía* is synonymous with *deslealtad, traición* (*disloyalty, treason*). (**Cometió una felonía con su mejor amigo.** He acted treacherously with his best friend.)

FELONY. Ya hemos dicho que en el catálogo de delitos hay muchas categorías, y designaciones diferentes entre el derecho napoleónico y el *common law*. *Felony* puede ser *delito mayor*, aunque evidentemente lo que cuenta son los delitos a que se aplica. (**His crime was defined as a felony.** La categoría de su delito es una felony.)

FÉRTIL. There are no special problems with translation into English.

FERTILE. En inglés se usa *fertile* y sus derivados para la idea de *fecundidad*, aunque empieza a emplearse el anglicismo. (**The infertile wife followed a treatment in order to become pregnant.** La esposa infecunda se sometió a un tratamiento para quedar embarazada.)

FEUDO. *Feudo* is a *fiefdom*, a territory owned by a local lord who exacts tribute and loyalty from his vassals. By extension, it applies to a situation in which someone exerts total dominance. (**La repostería es el feudo de los franceses.** Confectionery is the exclusive field of the French.)

FEUD. *Feud* quiere decir *enemistad, lucha de larga data*. (**The most famous feud in literary history is that of the Montagues and the Capulets.** La enemistad más famosa de la historia literaria es la de Montescos y Capuletos.)

FIESTA. *Fiesta* can be rendered as *party*, *festival* in the case of multitudinous celebrations, or in the case of *fiestas patronales*, as *patron saint's day*. (**Todo el pueblo asistió a la fiesta patronal.** The whole village joined in the patron saint's day festivities.)

FEAST. *Feast* es un festín o, en sentido figurado, algo maravilloso, como *a feast for the eyes*. (**The banquet table was a feast for the eyes.** Era maravilloso contemplar la mesa del banquete.)

FIGURA. The several meanings of these words match each other in the two languages.

FIGURE. En inglés, *figure*, aparte de los significados comunes, quiere decir *cifra*, *dígito*. (**The economic indicators showed promising figures.** Los indicadores económicos señalaban cifras promisorias.)

FIGURÍN. *Figurín* may be a *dandy*, a *pisaverde*. (**El actor de cine caminaba como figurín.** The movie actor moved around like a dandy.)

FIGURINE. *Figurine* es una *estatuilla*, una *modelo*. (**An ivory figurine fetched $20,000.** Una estatuilla de marfil recaudó $20.000.)

FIJAR. *Fijar* is to give permanence to something, to *establish*. (**El lema de la Real Academia de la Lengua Española es "fija, brilla y da esplendor."** The motto of the Royal Academy of the Spanish Language is: "it establishes, brightens and makes it resplendent.")

FIX. *To fix* también significa *reparar*, *conseguir una cita* o *disponer*. (**Fixing the car will cost more than the recovery price of a total loss.** Arreglar el coche costará más de lo que me darían si lo llevara a desguace. **Lucy wants me to fix her up with my friend John.** Lucy quiere que le consiga una cita con mi amigo John.)

Físico. *Físico* is *physicist.* **(Su profesión es la de físico atómico.** He is an atomic physicist by profession.) It also refers to the appearance, strength, or *physique* of a person. **(Tiene un físico de atleta.** He has an athlete's physique.)

Physician. Así como *chemical* no es necesariamente químico, *physician*, a diferencia de *physicist*, no significa *físico* sino médico. **(He had a good reputation as a physician.** Tenía buena reputación como médico.)

Fluido. The *fluido eléctrico* is referred to sometimes in the sense of *electricity.*

Fluid. Muy a menudo *fluid* significa *líquido*. **(To avoid constipation, you have to drink lots of fluids.** Hay que beber mucho líquido para evitar el estreñimiento.)

Formal. A person who is *formal* respects formalities and displays good manners in all his actions. **(Su pretendiente es muy formal.** Her suitor is very proper.)

Formal. Aplicado a papeles, documentos, gestiones, etc., *formal* quiere decir *oficial, conforme a los requisitos*, a diferencia de *informal*, que se traduce por *oficioso*. **(After informal contacts, a formal document was produced.** Tras los contactos oficiosos, se presentó un documento oficial.) *Formal wear* es una vestimenta elegante o de *ceremonias*. **(The invitation to the wedding said: formal wear.** La invitación a la boda hablaba de vestimenta de etiqueta.)

FORZADO, FORZOSO. *Trabajo forzado* (not *forzoso*) is *forced labor*. *Forzoso* means *compulsory, obligatory*. (**El avión con problemas realizó un aterrizaje forzoso en el primer aeropuerto disponible.** The plane in difficulty made a forced landing at the first available airport.)

FORCIBLE. Aparte de los significados comunes, *forcible* quiere decir *convincente*. (**He based his theory on a forcible argumentation.** Basó su teoría en un argumento convincente.)

FRACASO. No relation between the words. *Fracaso* is the contrary of success. (**El negocio fue un fracaso.** The enterprise was a failure [or a *flop*].)

FRACAS. *Fracas* es *alboroto, altercado, riña*. (**The fracas could be heard on the whole block.** El alboroto se sentía en toda la manzana.)

FRANQUICIA. *Franquicia* is a privilege, an exception from duties or a concession by a big manufacturer to sell their products on their conditions. (**Los diplomáticos tienen franquicia de importación sin impuestos.** Diplomats may import goods duty-free. **Varias cadenas de hamburgueserías venden franquicias en localidades pequeñas.** Several hamburger chains sell franchises in small villages.)

FRANCHISE. Las acepciones notadas a la izquierda son de reciente data relativamente en español (exención de derechos y concesión de sucursales). Algo más antigua es la noción de *derecho de votación* aplicado a un sector de la población. (**Women earned their franchise after a long struggle.** Las mujeres obtuvieron el derecho de votación tras una larga lucha.)

FRENTE. These words share the same meanings.

FRONT. Hay una película con la actuación de Woody Allen llamada *The Front*, que describe a un autor fracasado que se aviene a poner su nombre como *testaferro* en obras de autores incluidos en una lista negra política. El *front* sería lo que en el caso de políticos o autores literarios es el *negro*, que le escribe. *Véase Políticamente correcto.*

FRUICIÓN. *Fruición* is the special enjoyment produced by reading or watching a show, etc. (**Releyó con fruición las páginas de su libro favorito.** She enjoyed re-reading her favorite book.)

FRUITION. La culminación de un cometido es cuando éste alcanza *fruition*. (**The seven-year-old project just came to fruition last month.** Después de siete años, el proyecto culminó el mes pasado.)

FUENTE. In informatic systems, *fuente* is used for the English *font* to mean *tipo de letra*, *typeface*. The DRAE does not carry this meaning, an example of the unnecessary intrusion of a disguised foreign word.

FONT. Se designa así a un tipo de letra. (**Garamond and Bodoni created beautiful fonts of our alphabet.** Garamond y Bodoni crearon hermosos tipos de letra de nuestro alfabeto.)

GACETILLA. *Gacetilla* is a *flyer*, a short *prospectus,* or newspaper article. (**Los manifestantes repartían gacetillas con una lista de reivindicaciones.** The demonstrators distributed flyers with the list of their grievances and claims.)

GAZETEER. *Gazeteer* es un *índice*, habitualmente de *topónimos*, o un *callejero*. (**The atlas was supplemented with a gazeteer of place names.** El atlas se complementaba con un índice de lugares.)

GALANTE. *Galante* means *polite*, but also *flirtatious*. (**El joven galante bailó con casi todas las damas.** The flirtatious young man danced with almost all the ladies.)

GALLANT. Un hombre puede ser *gallant* si es *garboso, bien plantado, gallardo*. (**The young mother was proud of her gallant adolescent son.** La joven madre se enorgullecía de su hijo, un adolescente bien plantado.)

GAS. Words that apply to the different kinds of *gas* (*mineral, fuel* and even *body gases*) and also stand as an abbreviation of *gasoline*. (**Le recetaron un producto eficaz contra los gases.** He was prescribed an effective anti-gas product. **Agua mineral con gas.** Sparkling mineral water.)

GAS. Por ser *gas* abreviatura de *gasoline,* se dice *gas pedal*, o simplemente *gas*, para indicar el *acelerador* de un coche. (**He stepped on the gas of the Ferrari, and the car went like a flash.** Le dio al acelerador del Ferrari y el coche salió como una exhalación.) Queda por supuesto la acepción de combustible doméstico, *gas*, *natural gas* o *bottled gas* (gas envasado o en garrafas), según el caso. (**Some buses and taxis use CNG, that is, compressed natural gas.** Hay autobuses y taxis que usan gas natural comprimido.)

GASOLINA. Here lies a problem, both in English and in Spanish, in terms of usage. *Gasolina* may be the same product sold in different countries under the names *nafta*, *bencina*, or *keroseno*.

GASOLINE. Lo que en Estados Unidos se llama *gasolina* recibe en el Reino Unido el nombre de *petrol*.

GÉNERO. Here is a word with several meanings in Spanish, from a merely grammatical one to that of *the wares or articles sold by a merchant*. But the feminist movement at the end of the twentieth century has adopted *género* as a term with a sociological content, meaning *everything directed to the promotion of women and equality with men*. Linguistic conservatives have reacted negatively, in general because while not denying the justice of the fundamental struggle, they feel the existing language could be used in ways that reflect those ideas. (At the United Nations, where after some resistance the Spanish Language Service accepted the use of *género*, the French Service did not adopt a translation of the English *gender* and in all documents speaks of *"men and women," "the two sexes,"* or the *"equality of women,"* etc. To this writer, the whole question derives from an insidious intrusion of English, that considers *sex* as unpronounceable, which is not the case with Spanish. *See politically correct.*)

GENDER. Es común en los comités internacionales hablar de *mainstreaming of the gender perspective* (*incorporación de las consideraciones sobre la mujer y el hombre*, o de las diferencias de trato a ambos) en una politica, o presupuesto, o decisión, o la composición igualitaria, entre hombres y mujeres, de un parlamento o gabinete, por ejemplo. *Gender politics* tiene una amplia posible gama de aplicaciones. *Gender violence* o *domestic violence* (*violencia doméstica o de género*) se aplica exclusivamente a los maltratos a la mujer en el hogar, fuente hasta de asesinatos en muchos países. *Véase Políticamente correcto.*

GENIAL. In Spanish, something that is *genial* is the product of a superior mind or spirit. (**La invención de la red de internet ha sido genial.** The invention of the worldwide web has been marvelous.)

GENIAL. *Genial* en inglés quiere decir *de buen genio* o *talante.* (**With his genial disposition, he was always the life of the party.** Con su buen genio era siempre el alma de la fiesta.)

GENTIL. *Gentil* means courteous, good mannered. (**Gentil, era de maneras exquisitas.** He had the good manners of a gentleman.) *Gentil* also means *Gentile, non-Jewish.* (**Los judíos no pueden hacer prosélitos entre los gentiles.** Jews are prevented from proselitizing Gentiles.)

GENTEEL, GENTLE, GENTILE. Obviamente, tres palabras inglesas derivadas de la misma raíz, pero con matices diferentes de significado: *genteel* es *airoso, gallardo*; *gentle*, *suave, manso, tierno*; *gentile*, *pagano* o *no judío respecto de un judío.* (**Genteel, he was very popular with women.** Gallardo, era muy popular entre las mujeres. **He was a gentle soul.** Era un espíritu delicado. **Her religious family would not accept a gentile as her husband.** Su familia religiosa no aceptaría un gentil para marido.)

GLOBO. Words with common meanings, with the exception of *globo* as a toy or party adornment, translated as *balloon.* (**Para los cumpleaños de los niños, adornaban el salón con globos.** For the kids' birthdays, they decorated the room with balloons.)

GLOBE. Aparte de su significado geométrico, *globe* suele emplearse para definir el mundo, el *globo terráqueo.* (**That telephone system covers the entire globe.** Ese servicio telefónico abarca todo el mundo.)

GOL. This Hispanicized word (also called *tanto* in this specific case) is reserved for its meaning in football. (**El nuevo jugador hizo tres goles.** The new player scored three goals.)

GOAL. El goal del fútbol se llama así porque el balón llega a su *objetivo*, el arco o la puerta. (**The production team achieved the set goal.** El equipo de producción cumplió el objetivo estipulado.)

GRÁCIL, GRACIOSO. The same etymology, specific meanings. *Grácil* is *slender, fine.* (**Era de grácil silueta.** She had a slender figure.) *Gracioso* means *witty.* (**La obra estaba llena de salidas graciosas.** The play was full of witty remarks.) *A título gracioso* means *free.*

GRACEFUL, GRACIOUS. *Graceful* es *agraciado, garboso.* (**The graceful dancer won the admiration of the public.** La grácil bailarina era la admiración del público.) *Gracious* puede aplicarse a un soberano o a un favor o servicio. (**Her gracious majesty.** Su graciosa majestad. **He graciously donated his work at the benefit.** Hizo graciosa donación de su trabajo en el beneficio.)

GRANADA. *Granada*, the fruit, is a *pomegranate.* (**La granada tiene un sabor peculiar.** The pomegranate has a peculiar taste.) *Granada* can also mean *grenade.*

GRENADE. *Grenade* es un arma, un proyectil llamado *granada* en español. (**The insurgents threw grenades at the United States military trucks.** Los insurgentes arrojaron granadas a los carros militares de los Estados Unidos.)

GRATIFICACIÓN, GRATIFICAR. *Gratificación* is a *prize*, a *reward* or a *bonus.* (**Una vez firmado el contrato, los negociadores recibieron una gratificación.** When the contract was signed, the negotiators received a bonus.)

GRATIFY, GRATIFICATION. *Gratification* es *satisfacción, complacencia.* (**People in general expressed gratification at the positive attitude of the government.** La poblacion en general expresó complacencia ante la actitud positiva del gobierno.)

GRATUIDAD. *Gratuidad* is the fact of something being free of charge. (**La gratuidad es garantía de la educación primaria para todos.** A free elementary education is a guarantee of schooling for everybody.)

GRATUITY. *Gratuity* es la *propina*. (**Sometimes a 15% gratuity is automatically added to your restaurant bill.** A veces se añade automáticamente un 15% de propina a la cuenta del restaurante.)

GRAVE. *Grave* has in English and in Spanish the meanings of *serious, solemn, of very delicate health*. And in Spanish words stressed on the penultimate syllable are called *graves*. (**En español, las palabras graves llevan acento escrito si no terminan en n, s o vocal.** In Spanish, words stressed on the penultimate syllable take an accent only if they do not end in n, s or a vowel.)

GRAVE. En ingles y español coinciden las distintas acepciones de esta palabra. Además, *grave* es *tumba*. (**An unmarked grave.** Una tumba no identificada.)

GUARDIÁN. *Guardián* refers to a *warden, protector* or *defender*. (**El guardián de prisión realiza un trabajo peligroso.** The prison warden has a dangerous job. **Los censores se tienen por guardianes de la moral pública.** Censors consider themselves as the guardians of public morality.)

GUARDIAN. *Guardian* es un término que se utiliza para varias actividades, que pueden ser de *celador, sereno* o *tutor*. (**The judge named a guardian for the orphan.** El juez designó un tutor para el huérfano.)

GUERRILLA. In Spanish, this word designates an irregular force, whose members are *guerrilleros*. (**La guerrilla se desplazó más al norte.** The guerrillas went north.)

GUERRILLA. En inglés, se suele designar como *guerrilla* a un miembro individal de esta milicia. (**A guerrilla fighter was wounded in the operation.** Un guerrillero resultó herido en la operación.)

HESITAR. *Hesitar (hesitate, vacillate)* exists in Spanish, but is rarely used. It may also mean *to stutter*. (**Cuanto más pensaba en la inversión, más hesitaba en hacerla.** The more he thought about investing, the more he hesitated.)

HESITATE. Las acepciones más comunes de *to hesitate* son *dudar, vacilar*. (**He hesitated to invest in the Stock Exchange.** Dudaba si invertir en la Bolsa de Valores.)

HONESTO, HONESTIDAD. (**La mujer del César no sólo debe ser honesta sino parecerlo.** Caesar's wife must not only be honest but she must look it. **La honestidad es la mejor política comercial.** Honesty is the best policy.)

HONEST, HONESTY. *Honest* es *honesto, honrado*, pero también quiere decir *puro, sin mezcla.* (**He earns an honest living.** Se gana la vida honradamente. **This product is honest veal.** Este es un producto puro de ternera.) *Honest to God* equivale a *una promesa, un juramento.*

HONORABLE. *Honorable* means *worthy of being honored*. It has become a formal way of addressing authority, in the executive, the legislative and the judiciary. (**El Honorable José Pérez, presidente del Senado.** Honorable José Pérez, president of the Senate.)

HONORABLE. *Honorable* puede traducirse también por *ilustre, honorífico, respetable.* (**He is an honorable member of his profession.** Es un miembro ilustre de su profesión.)

Humano, Humanitario. The *human body* translates el *cuerpo humano*. *Derechos humanos* is an expression nobody challenges. **(Los derechos humanos son de interés fundamental para la ONU.** Human rights are of fundamental concern to the UN.) *Humanitario* refers to *human rights*, the *derecho humanitario* covering legislation protecting or regulating human rights. **(El derecho humanitario internacional se enseña en la escuela secundaria.** International humanitarian law is taught in high school.)

Human, Humane, Humanitarian. La expresión *human rights* ya está consagrada, al punto que se ha olvidado su origen **(Droits de l'homme et du citoyen,** en francés, o sea **los derechos del hombre y del ciudadano),** ya que se adujo que *human* comprendía al hombre y a la mujer (políticamente correcto). *Humane* es *humanitario* y, por extensión, *considerado.* **(Prisioners should receive humane treatment.** Debe darse a los presos un trato humanitario. **Humanitarian international law.** Derecho humanitario internacional.)

Humor. Equivalent words in their normal meaning.

Humor. *To humor,* en lenguaje familiar, quiere decir *complacer, seguir la corriente.* **(She humored his idea to bike cross-country.** Le complació en cuanto a recorrer el lugar en bicicleta.)

Idioma. *Idioma* is translated as *language* or *tongue,* never as *idiom.* **(Hay muchos idiomas minoritarios en África.** There are many minority languages in Africa.)

Idiom. *Idiom* es una expresión idiomática o una *jerga* o manera particular de hablar. **(Many English idioms defy literal translation.** En inglés hay muchos modismos que no admiten traducción literal. **The idiom of the underworld is for the initiated.** La jerga de los bajos fondos sólo la entienden los iniciados.)

IGNORAR. *Ignorar* means not to know something. (**Se ignora el sitio preciso del mundo en que apareció el hombre.** The exact place of the world where man appeared is not known.)

IGNORE. *To ignore* no es desconocer algo sino *hacer caso omiso* de algo o alguien. (**The sick man ignored the recommendations of his doctor.** El enfermo hizo caso omiso de las recomendaciones de su médico.)

ILUSIÓN, DELUSIÓN. These terms should not be confused. *Ilusión* is the exact equivalent of *illusion,* while *delusion*, a psychiatric term, is already found in the academic literature as *delusión* in Spanish. (**La delusión es una evasión de la realidad.** Delusion is an escape from reality.)

ILLUSION, DELUSION. *Delusion* es *delirio* o falsa concepción de los hechos o las cosas. (**His delusion was to think that he was a great scientist.** Tenía la delusión de ser un gran hombre de ciencia.)

ILUSTRAR. As in the case of *edificar* o *educar*, these words have also a figurative meaning. *Ilustrar* originally means *to exemplify something with images*. Figuratively it means *to educate* or *to inform*. (**Lo ilustró sobre el plan.** He informed him about the plan.)

ILLUSTRATE. Se aplica aquí lo dicho en *edify* o *educate*. Como en el caso de *edify* o *educate*, *illustrate* tiene un sentido figurado: *aclarar* o *demostrar algo*. (**The salesman illustrated the operation of the appliance.** El vendedor le demostró el funcionamiento del aparato.)

IMAGEN. DRAE defines *imagen pública* as the characteristics that a person or entity has in the eyes of the community. This may well be the justification of the expression *asesor de imagen*, the specialist who tries to improve the presentation, the *carisma* of a politician.

IMAGE. En general, las dos palabras son equivalentes.

IMPACTO. The original meaning of *impacto* is *the mark left by a collision of two objects*. (**El impacto del mísil en el muro podía aún verse.** You could still see where the missile hit the wall.) But in current use it has come to mean *the repercussion or consequence of something*.

IMPACT. *Impact es la marca dejada por un arma en cierta superficie.* El uso ha hecho que su sentido se extienda al de *efectos*, *repercusiones*, palabras preferibles para la traducción. (**The impact of the new law has yet to be seen.** Quedan aún por verse los efectos de la nueva legislación.)

IMPREGNABLE. In Spanish, this word, a synonym of *unsaturable*, means *permeable*, capable of being penetrated, also in a figurative sense. (**Era impregnable a las ideas nuevas.** He was receptive to new ideas.)

IMPREGNABLE. La palabra inglesa tiene un sentido muy distinto de la española: quiere decir *inexpugnable*, *inconquistable*. (**The castle was an impregnable fortress.** El castillo era una fortaleza inexpugnable.)

IMPÚDICO. *Impúdico* means *immodest*. (**Lo arrestaron por gestos impúdicos en la calle.** He was arrested for immodest gestures in the street.)

IMPUDENT. *Impudent* tiene la acepción de *descarado*, *atrevido*. (**The impudent boy refused to listen to his mother.** El niño descarado se negó a escuchar a su madre.)

INCONSISTENTE. *See consistente.*

INCONSISTENT.

INCONVENIENTE. In Spanish, this word has a wide range of meanings, implying *bothersome*, *inappropriate*. (**Las disposiciones tomadas eran decididamente inconvenientes.** The arrangements were definitely inappropriate.)

INCONVENIENT. No hay diferencia esencial entre los dos términos. (**He had an inconvenient encounter on his way to work.** Tuvo un encuentro desagradable camino al trabajo.)

INCORPORAR. *Incorporarse* means *to get up.* (**Se incorporó de un salto al oir la noticia.** She jumped at the news.) It also means *to form part of, or be associated with, an organization.* (**En la Argentina, hay colegios privados incorporados al régimen de los públicos.** In Argentina, there are private schools associated with public ones.)

INCORPORATE. En derecho estadounidense, *to incorporate* es *constituir una sociedad mediante su registro ante la autoridad competente.* (**Small businesses prefer to incorporate in order to operate with limited liability and enjoy the protection of the law.** Las pequeñas empresas prefieren lograr su registro, para funcionar con responsabilidad limitada y gozar de la protección de la ley.) También una localidad o pueblo *is incorporated*, igualmente para garantizar su estatus en la provincia o comarca respectiva.

INDIGNANTE. *Indignante* is whatever produces indignation. (**Es indignante enterarse de las fortunas de los dirigentes corruptos.** The fact that corrupt leaders have great fortunes is cause for indignation.)

INDIGNANT. *Indignant* es *indignado*, no que causa indignación. (**The black man was indignant when his customer made a biased remark.** El negro se sintió indignado cuando su cliente hizo una observación discriminatoria.)

INDISCRETO. *Indiscreto* is the perfect equivalent of *indiscreet.*

INDISCREET, INDISCRETE. La ligera diferencia ortográfica entre *indiscreet* e *indiscrete* justifica dos sentidos diferentes. (**The next door neighbor was an indiscreet gossip**. La vecina de al lado era una charlatana indiscreta. **An indiscrete flow of ideas characterized his speech.** Un continuo fluir de ideas caracterizaba su discurso.)

INDUCIR. In Spanish, the meaning of this verb is limited to the idea of exercising influence to do something. (**Lo indujo a participar en el concurso.** He convinced him to participate in the contest.)

INDUCE. No sólo *inducir*, sino *causar*, *producir* pueden expresarse en inglés con este verbo. (**The change in the high and low atmospheric pressures in the atmosphere induced climatic variations.** Los cambios en el comportamiento de las zonas de alta y baja presión de la atmósfera provocaron los cambios climáticos.)

INDUSTRIOSO. *Industrioso* is *talented, resourceful*. (**El guardián es muy industrioso en los arreglos del edificio.** The custodian is very resourceful in all the repairs of the building.)

INDUSTRIOUS. *Industrious* también quiere decir *aplicado, diligente*. (**The new office boy is so industrious that he will surely climb to higher positions.** El nuevo cadete de la oficina es tan diligente que seguramente ascenderá a puestos más elevados.)

INFAME. A person who is an *infame* is *vile, despicable*. (**Se comportó como un infame con su mejor amigo.** His behavior with his best friend was despicable.)

INFAMOUS. *Infamous* quiere decir *vergonzoso, ignominioso* o se aplica a quien tiene una mala reputación. (**The infamous politician was not re-elected.** El politico poco respetable no fue reelegido.)

INFLAMABLE. *Inflamable* is something that can easily catch fire. (**Es una sustancia muy inflamable.** It is a highly flammable substance.)

FLAMMABLE, INFLAMMABLE. The Penguin Dictionary explica que las palabras *flammable* e *inflammable*, aparentemente contradictorias, significan lo mismo, y que ante el temor de la confusión provocada por el prefijo *in* conviene emplear *flammable*, así como *nonflammable* para su opuesto, *incombustible*.

INFORMALIDAD. *Informalidad* is the lack of manners, *incivility*. (**Por su informalidad, sus amigos ya no lo esperan.** He is not reliable with appointments, and his friends do not wait for him anymore.)

INFORMALITY. Por *informality* se entiende la *falta de ceremonias*, de pautas sociales muy conservadoras. (**It was an enjoyable party, especially because of its informality.** La fiesta gustó mucho, particularmente por su poca solemnidad.)

INFORMANTE. *Informante* is one who reports. (**El miembro informante de la comisión presentó su dictamen.** The reporting member of the committee introduced his submission.) In parliamentary language, *ponente* is also used.

INFORMER. Muy específico es un *informer* (*delator*). (**During the McCarthy era, well-known showbusiness people informed on colleagues.** Durante la época de McCarthy, muchos famosos del espectáculo delataron a colegas.)

INGENIERO. *Ingeniero* is reserved in Spanish for university graduates in different specializations, but not for technicians with a lower education. (**Sólo los ingenieros están habilitados para concebir y dirigir la construcción de viviendas.** Only engineers are allowed to design and oversee the construction of houses.)

ENGINEER. En los Estados Unidos, *engineer* suele aplicarse a *técnicos, incluso personal calificado* en ciertas disciplinas que requieren una licencia municipal como electricista, conductor del metro, fontanero, técnico de sonido, etc., además de los diplomados universitarios. (**Many sound engineers become disk jockeys.** Muchos técnicos de sonido actúan de mezcladores de música en discotecas.)

INGENUIDAD. *Ingenuidad* means *naivete*. (**Con ingenuidad hay quien cree que con "su sistema" ganará a la ruleta.** There are those who naively believe that their "system" will allow them to win at roulette.)

INGENUITY. *Ingenuity* es el *genio*, la *capacidad de innovar* en una técnica o industria. (**After World War II Japanese industry began to imitate Western products, but then applied their ingenuity to innovate.** Tras la segunda guerra mundial, la industria japonesa comenzó imitando los productos occidentales, pero luego aplicó su ingenio a la innovación.)

INHABITABLE. These are two opposite concepts. In the Spanish word *inhabitable*, *in-* is a negative prefix. (**Una gran porción del país es inhabitable por desértica.** A substantial portion of the country cannot be inhabited because it is a desert.)

INHABITABLE. En inglés, *to inhabit* es *habitar*, de modo que *inhabitable* es *habitable*. (**For new buildings, the municipality must determine if they are inhabitable.** Los edificios nuevos deben tener un certificado de habitabilidad del ayuntamiento.)

INJURIA, INJURIAR, INJURIOSO. *Una injuria* is an *insult, a defamatory remark*. *Injuriar*, consequently, is to *insult, offend, abuse*. (**Se sintió injuriado al ser comparado con el famoso delincuente.** He felt insulted at being compared with the notorious criminal.)

INJURE, INJURY, INJURIOUS. *To injure* significa *herir, injury, herida*. (**He only suffered minor injuries in the crash.** El choque sólo le produjo heridas leves. **To add insult to injury.** Sobre llovido, mojado.) *Injurious* es *perjudicial*. (**The project is injurious to the neighborhood.** El proyecto es perjudicial para el barrio.)

INMODESTO. *Inmodesto* in Spanish is the opposite of *modest*. (**Hacía inmodestamente una relación de sus virtudes.** Without humility, he listed all his qualities.)

IMMODEST. En su uso más corriente, ***immodest*** quiere decir *impúdico, indecoroso*. (**The new play, with its explicit sex scenes, is too immodest for my taste.** La nueva obra, con sus escenas de carácter sexual muy evidente, me resulta demasiado indecorosa.)

INQUISICIÓN. In DRAE *inquisición* is used only in connection with the infamous Tribunal del Santo Oficio, and with ***averiguación***. The Diccionario del Español Actual, of the academician Manuel Seco and others, also lists *tyranny, abuse of power*, as other meanings of ***inquisición***.

INQUISITION. The Penguin Dictionary define ***inquisition*** como una investigación o examen *despiadado* o *implacable* (***ruthless***), adjetivo que también emplea para ***inquisitorial***.

INSENSIBLE. In Spanish, *insensible* defines someone who does not show his feelings. (**Se mostraba insensible ante los sufrimientos de los colegas.** He was insensitive to suffering colleagues.)

INSENSIBLE, INSENSITIVE. *Insensible* es alguien que no es capaz de percibir algo por los sentidos: *inconsciente, inanimado*. (**The patient was insensible to stimulation.** El paciente no respondía a los estímulos.) *Insensitive* es el equivalente español de *insensible*, que no responde a estímulos emocionales o estéticos. (**He was insensitive to his friend's loss.** Se mostró insensible a la pérdida de su amigo.)

INSTANCIA. In both languages, it means *a tribunal* of a certain level or a *petition*. (**El demandante perdió su reclamación en primera instancia.** The claimant lost his case in first instance. **Elevó una instancia a la Dirección de Migraciones.** He sent a petition to the immigration authorities.)

INSTANCE. El significado que no se da en español es el de *caso o ejemplo*. (**For instance, this was a case of double meaning.** Por ejemplo, este fue un caso de doble sentido.)

INSTRUIR. *Instruir* is equivalent to *educar*. (**Un pueblo instruido es el capital de una nación.** An educated people is the nation's capital.)

INSTRUCT. *To instruct* significa *dar instrucciones, encomendar, encargar*. (**The Secretary General was instructed to report on the implementation of the policy.** Se encomendó al Secretario General que informara sobre la puesta en práctica de la política.)

INTELIGENCIA. *En la inteligencia de algo* means *on the understanding that*. (**Aprobaremos esto en la inteligencia de que no creará un precedente.** We will approve this on the understanding that it will not create a precedent.)

INTELLIGENCE. Idea que el uso ya ha incorporado al habla corriente: *intelligence* como espionaje, actividad encubierta para obtener información secreta. (**The government learned about the planned attacks from their intelligence gathered in several countries.** El gobierno se enteró de los ataques planeados por inteligencia recogida en varios países.)

INTENTAR. *Intentar* is *to try*. (**El nadador intentó batir el récord mundial.** The swimmer tried to beat the world record.)

INTEND. El verbo inglés *to intend* significa *proponerse*. (**This year I intend to travel to Germany.** Este año me propongo viajar a Alemania.)

INTERACTIVO. *See proactivo.*

INTERACTIVE.

ÍNTERIN. *En el ínterin* means *in the meantime.* (**Esperaba la llegada del tren, y en el ínterin pasó un amigo.** He was waiting for the train to come, and in the meantime a friend came.)

INTERIM. *Interim* es *provisional, transitorio.* (**After the coup d'état, an interim government was formed.** Después del golpe de Estado, se formó un gobierno provisional.)

INTIMACIÓN. *Intimación* is *a notification to someone to appear before an authority or to do something ordered by a judge or the police.* (**Recibió una intimación a presentarse ante el juez.** He was urgently summoned to appear before the judge.)

INTIMATION. Una *intimation* es una *insinuación, sospecha* o *indirecta.* (**He had an intimation that such a thing would happen.** Tenía la sospecha de que eso ocurriría.)

INTIMAR. *Intimar* is *to become intimate.* (**En poco tiempo intimaron.** In no time they became intimate.) Also, it means *to notify urgently to appear.* (**El comisario intimó al infractor a presentarse a la policía.** The chief of police urgently ordered the transgressor to come to the station.)

INTIMATE. *To intimate* es *dar a entender,* revelar con medias palabras. (**The boss intimated that he was thinking of a reorganization.** El patrón dio a entender que pensaba hacer una reorganización.)

INTOXICAR. *Intoxicar* is used in Spanish for any kind of poisoning by toxins. (**El pescado en mal estado la intoxicó.** Bad fish poisoned her.) In a figurative sense, it is used to denote bad influences. (**Las sectas lo intoxicaron hasta hacerle perder la cabeza.** Sects poisoned him until he lost his head.)

INTOXICATE. El uso en Estados Unidos ha hecho que el verbo *to intoxicate* se use específicamente para la intoxicación por alcohol, o *ebriedad*, como DWI (*driving while intoxicated*/conducir ebrio) or DUI (*driving under the influence*/alcohol o drogas).

INTRODUCIR. *Introducir* is not used in Spanish with the sense of *to make presentations among people*. (**Introdujo la moneda en la alcancía.** He put the coin in the piggy bank.)

INTRODUCE. *To introduce* es *hacer una presentación.* (**I wish to introduce my friend, Mr. Pérez.** Quiero presentarle a mi amigo, el Sr. Pérez.)

INVERTIR. *Invertir* means in Spanish both *invert*, or *revert*, and *invest*. (**Invertir en bolsa no ha resultado tan rendidor como hacerlo en inmobiliaria.** To invest in the Stock Exchange was not as profitable as in real estate.)

INVERT, INVEST. *Invert* es *invertir, volver al revés.* *Invest* significa *invertir*, y además *instalar en un cargo, conferir una dignidad, sitiar una plaza.* (**Now roles are inverted and he is in charge of cooking.** Ahora, los papeles se han invertido, él está a cargo de la cocina. **He invested in bonds.** Invirtió en bonos. **The winner of the election was invested President.** El triunfador en las elecciones recibió la investidura de Presidente.)

Israelí, Israelita. Sometimes the two words are confused, and in some papers *judíos* is even used to mean *Israelíes*. The *judíos* (*Jews*) may be citizens of different countries, and it would be as erroneous to use *judío* for *Israeli* as it would for a *Catholic* to be called *Vatican* or something of the sort. At present, **Hebreo** is mostly restricted to the language. (**Los israelíes hablan hebreo, hay israelíes judíos y árabes.** Israelis speak Hebrew. There are Jewish and Arab Israelis.)

Israeli, Israelite. *Israelite* significa descendiente de Israel. La diferencia entre **Israeli** e **Israelite** estriba en que el primer término designa una nacionalidad y el segundo una religion. (**The Israelite community in Brooklyn is very strong.** La comunidad judía de Brooklyn es muy numerosa. **Foreigners whose mother is Jewish may acquire Israeli citizenship.** Los extranjeros de madre judía pueden obtener la ciudadanía israelí.)

Jornada. *Jornada* means *the work done during a day*. (**La jornada de trabajo no puede exceder de ocho horas.** A day's work cannot exceed eight hours.)

Journey. *Journey* es *cualquier viaje por tierra* (**voyage**, por mar). No tiene por qué limitarse a un día, puede ser de más o menos. (**His journey included several European countries.** En su viaje atravesó varios países europeos.)

Jubilación. *Jubilación* (or **retiro**) means *retirement* and the consequent *pension*. (**Obtuvo una buena jubilación después de 25 años de trabajo.** He got a good pension after 25 years of work.)

Jubilation. *Jubilation* es *júbilo, regocijo*. (**The fans greeted the victory of their local team with great jubilation.** Jubilosamente recibieron los adictos la victoria del equipo local.)

Justicia. The two terms have the same meaning.

Justice. En los Estados Unidos, *justice* es un juez, que puede serlo del Tribunal Supremo o de jurisdicciones incluso inferiores, como *justice of the peace* (*juez de paz*).

LABOR. *Labor* means a *fine piece of crafted work in fabric, lace, etc.* In olden times, the occupation of women in Spain was given as *Sus labores*, meaning *Her tasks at home.* (**Era una fina labor de encaje.** That was a fine piece of lace work.)

LABOR. *Labor* quiere decir varias cosas en inglés: a veces *trabajo* (*Love's Labour Lost*/Trabajos de amor perdidos), y también *mano de obra, Partido Laborista, estar dando a luz.* (**Capital and labor should work in harmony.** El capital y la mano de obra deben actuar en armonía. **Labor won the last elections.** El Partido Laborista ganó las últimas elecciones. **She is in labor.** Está por dar a luz.)

LAGUNA. *Laguna* is a *small lake.* (**Dentro de su propiedad había una laguna.** There was a small lake on his property.)

LAGOON. *Lagoon* no es laguna sino *albufera.* (**On the way to Nimes, in the south of France, we pass a lagoon.** Camino de Nimes, en el sur de Francia, pasamos por una albufera.)

LARGO. *Largo* is *long* and not *large.* (**Cayó en la calle cuan largo era.** He fell full length on the street.)

LARGE. Ya dijimos en *enlarge* que *large* no significa *largo.* (**There is a large strip of cultivated land by the canal.** Hay una ancha faja de tierra de cultivo junto al canal. **These shoes are too large.** Estos zapatos son demasiado grandes.)

LATINO. *See **American**.*

LATIN.

LECTURA. *Lectura* can be rendered as *reading.* (**La lectura de la ponencia resultó aburrida.** The reading of the communication was quite boring.)

LECTURE. *Lecture* es una conferencia, una disertación académica. (**The scholar gave his lecture before a full house.** El académico pronunció su disertación ante una sala llena.)

LEGAL. *Legal* means *according to the law*. (**La edad legal del matrimonio para los chicos es de 18 años.** The legal age for marriage for boys is 18.)

LEGAL. El adjetivo *legal* significa *jurídico*, relacionado con el derecho, no necesariamente *legal* o *legítimo*. (**The legal status of the document is in doubt.** Es dudosa la condicion jurídica del documento. **It is legal to stop here.** Es legal [está permitido] detenerse aquí.)

LEGALIZAR, LEGÍTIMO, LEGITIMAR. *Legalizar* means *to have something authenticated*. (**Los documentos de exportación deben ser legalizados en el consulado.** Export papers must be authenticated at the consulate. **Al casarse, legitimó a su hijo natural.** He legitimated his natural son with his marriage.)

LEGITIMATE. Como adjetivo, *legitimate* significa además de legítimo o lícito, *válido, auténtico, cierto,* y como verbo *aprobar, autorizar.* (**He had a legitmate reason to act as he did.** Tuvo una razón válida para obrar de ese modo. **With his signature, he legitimated the permit.** Autorizó el permiso con su firma.)

LENGUAJE. *Lenguaje* is used for many forms of communication: *sign, flower,* even *cybernetic.* (**Hay intérpretes del lenguaje gestual.** There are interpreters of sign language.)

LANGUAGE. *Language* se traduce por *idioma* o *lengua* si se trata del habla de un país. (**Many minority languages are in danger of extinction.** Muchos idiomas minoritarios están en riesgo de extinción.)

LENGUAJE FIGURADO, LENGUAJE
GRÁFICO. In Spanish and English,
the popular and literary usage
of proverbs and quotations is
widespread. English probably
makes more frequent use of
what I call "graphic" language,
the utilization of images that are
difficult to render literally, let
alone in their intended sense:

a pan y agua. With very
little sustenance, as in a jail
(just bread and water).

a vuelo de pájaro. With
a panoramic view.

capicúa. From Catalan:
head and tail.

*luchar contra molinos de
viento*. Taken from Quixote:
to face imaginary enemies.

matar dos pájaros de un tiro.
To kill two birds with one stone.

para vestir santos. Remain
unmarried, going only to church.

quinta columna. Fifth column.
First used by a Franco general
who said he had Madrid encircled
during the war by four columns,
and that a fifth one consisting of
his loyals was working inside
the city. Denotes a clandestine
group helping the enemy.

trabajo negro. Moonlighting.

una mano atrás y otra adelante.
Like immigrants, without
anything of value, just hands
to cover their front and back.

FIGURATIVE LANGUAGE. Llamo
lenguaje "gráfico" o figurado al
uso de expresiones que dan una
imagen de su sentido. En algunos
casos proceden de la literatura,
pero muchas se han desarrollado
popularmente, muchas tienen su
origen en el deporte y a veces los
paralelos son difíciles de descubrir.

Algunos ejemplos de imágenes
en inglés:

armchair strategist. El que desde
un cómodo punto de observación
pontifica lo que debería hacerse en
una situación, por lo general difícil.

as the crow flies. La distancia
en línea recta, incluso
imaginaria, no por el camino
o medio de transporte.

at arm's length. Bien alejado.

back-seat driver. Quien
da instrucciones sin ser
responsable de una acción.

back to back. Se dice de
dos acciones seguidas, sin
solución de continuidad.

beeline. Directo.

big brother. Expresión debida
a George Orwell, que en su
obra *1984* describió un mundo
tiránico en que el "hermano
mayor" vigilaba a todos.

black-listed. Censurado,
prohibido, vetado, sin defensa.

FIGURATIVE LANGUAGE *(Continued)*

bottom line. Originariamente se refiere a la cifra final de resultados de un balance. Se aplica al beneficio final, o al costo total.

brain-drain. Éxodo de profesionales, por lo general de países en desarrollo a países industrializados, traducido a veces por fuga de cerebros o de materia gris.

brainstorming. Suele ser una reunión de hombres de negocios o ejecutivos en que se barajan toda suerte de alternativas, hasta las más absurdas, para llegar a una decisión sobre estrategia o plan comercial.

business as usual. O sea, sin cambios, sin innovar, a la antigua.

busman's holiday. Volver a lo que se hace siempre, como el chofer que descansa conduciendo su automóvil.

double dipping. "Mojar dos veces en la salsa", o gozar ilegalmente de una doble ventaja a partir de un único recurso.

fine print. Condiciones ocultas de un contrato o acuerdo.

free ride. Disfrutar de algo sin merecerlo, aprovechar algo más de una vez.

iron curtain. Expresión debida a Churchill, quien dijo, refiriéndose al este comunista, que un telón de acero había caído sobre Europa.

Figurative language *(Continued)*

lame duck. Político a punto de terminar su mandato y que no ha sido reelegido.

Monday-morning quarterback. Lo mismo que *armchair strategist*. Alude al hincha de un equipo que, al día siguiente del partido, explica lo que debió hacerse en el campo de juego para ganarlo.

moonlighting. Hacer trabajo negro.

one size fits all. Querer aplicar la misma solución a situaciones muy distintas.

pigeon hole. Casillero, por la similitud con un palomar.

rain check. Hacer valer un beneficio, visita, espectáculo, en una nueva ocasión por no poder realizarse en la primera.

red tape. Burocracia, por las cintas de los legajos.

rubber necking. En los Estados Unidos, se suele retrasar la regularización del tráfico en el lugar de un accidente porque los automovilistas disminuyen la velocidad para echar una ojeada al costado, torciendo el cuello como si fuera de goma.

stone's throw. A muy poca distancia.

straitjacket. Restricción extrema.

u-turn. Retorno, vuelta en 180 grados.

FIGURATIVE LANGUAGE *(Continued)*
wildcat (strike). (Huelga) sorpresiva.

window dressing. Hermosear algo.

window shopping. Detenerse a ver las vidrieras de una tienda, "comprando" con la mirada.

LETRA. *Letra* may mean the *lyrics* of a song. (**Las letras de muchas canciones francesas son de conocidos poetas.** Well-known poets wrote the lyrics of many French songs.) In olden times, when physical punishment was common in schools, it was said *La letra con sangre entra* (literally, *instruction works with blood*).

LETTER. En *letter of credit*, letter se traduce por *carta*. *The letter and the spirit of the law* alude al texto de una norma, que debe aplicarse según el espíritu que informó su dictado. (**Not always does the letter of a law convey its spirit.** No siempre un texto legal responde a su intención.)

LIBRERÍA. *Librería* is both *bookstore* and *bookshelf*. For the latter, the term most used in Latin America for library is *biblioteca*, which also refers to a book series or collection. (**En su librería tenían lugar preferente las obras de la Biblioteca de Ideas Contemporáneas.** On his bookshelf, the titles of the Contemporary Ideas Series held pride of place.)

LIBRARY. *Library* es *biblioteca*; unido a algunas palabras se utiliza para designar determinadas colecciones: por ejemplo, *record library*, *discoteca*; *newspaper library*, *hemeroteca*. (**The classical music station had a record library of enormous value.** La discoteca de la radio clásica tenía un gran valor. **The newspaper library was always consulted by historians.** La hemeroteca siempre era consultada por los historiadores.)

LIBRERO. *Librero* is a *bookseller*, or the owner of a bookshop or bookstore. (**Un buen librero debe conocer los autores que promueve.** A good bookseller knows about the authors he promotes.)

LIBRARIAN. Aunque es elemental, cabe puntualizar que un *librarian* es un *bibliotecario*. (**Apart from being cultivated, a librarian must be conversant with universal book classification.** Además de poseer cultura general, el bibliotecario debe conocer la clasificación bibliográfica universal.)

LICENCIA. *Licencia* has several meanings in common with *license*, and especially in Latin America, it means *permiso* in employment, applied to annual holidays, *maternity leave, unpaid leave*, etc. (*licencia por vacaciones anuales, licencia de maternidad, licencia sin haberes*). (**Los funcionarios públicos tienen derecho a 30 días de licencia anual.** Government employees are entitled to 30 days of leave per year.)

LICENSE. Puede referirse cualquiera de los dos términos a la matrícula de un coche o a un permiso en general. (**Cars with odd license plate numbers could not be driven on even dates.** Automóviles con matrículas impares no podían circular en días pares. **Granting him a driver's license is giving him a license to kill.** Otorgarle un permiso de conductor equivale a darle permiso para matar.) En sentido figurado *license* significa *libertinaje*. (**Permissiveness does not mean license.** La libertad de obrar no significa libertinaje.)

LICOR. *Licor* and *liquor* are both generic. In a figurative sense, they are also used to mean something *delicious*, like in the expression *licor de los dioses, gods' delight.* (**Más que zumo es un licor**. It is more than juice, it is liquor.)

LIQUOR, LIQUEUR. *Liquor* es la designación genérica de las bebidas con alcohol; *liqueur* el licor dulce que se toma como aperitivo o de postre. (**In New York, only liquor stores may sell alcoholic beverages.** En Nueva York, sólo las tiendas de bebidas alcohólicas pueden venderlas. **Several brands of liqueurs were originally manufactured in religious establishments.** Varios tipos de licores se empezaron a fabricar en sitios religiosos.)

LILA, LIRIO. The Spanish word *lila* means *lilac*. (**Vestía un traje color lila.** She wore a lilac suit.) *Lirio* is *lily* (*lirio del valle*, *lily of the valley*).

LILY. *Lily* suele usarse en el sentido de *blanco, puro* o *delicado*. (**She is a lily of a girl.** Es una niña pura.)

LOCAL. As a noun, *local* is the term for a closed environment. (**Un local amplio para fiestas.** A large place appropriate for parties.)

LOCAL. En los Estados Unidos, *local* puede designar la *rama de un gremio*. (**The strike was called for by local 231, machinists.** Convocó la huelga la sección 231, de maquinistas.)

LOTE. Referring to land, *lote* is a *plot*. (**Compró un lote en un barrio nuevo, con ánimo de edificar su casa.** He bought a plot in a new neighborhood, with the intention of building his house.)

LOT. Hay varios significados asociados a esta palabra inglesa: puede ser un *lote* o grupo de cosas, denotar una *gran cantidad*. (**In the auction, lot 21 included lots of bric-a-brac.** En la subasta, el lote 21 estaba constituido por un montón de chucherías.)

MAGNETO. *Magneto* describes a *generator*, used most frequently in combustion engines. (**Había un fallo en el magneto del coche.** There was some problem with the car generator.)

MAGNET. Una acepción de *magnet* es *imán*. (**In her kitchen, magnets hold reminders.** En su cocina hay recordatorios, asegurados con imanes.)

MALL. *Galería de compras*, por otro nombre inglés. *Véase* **Shopping.**

MANEJAR. *Manejar* is *to handle, manipulate*, and in some countries it is used for *to drive*. (**Maneja bien las situaciones complicadas.** He handles complex situations very well. **Manejó el coche todo el día.** He drove the car all day.)

MANAGE. *To manage* es *administrar, dirigir, arreglárselas*. (**His accountant managed his investments.** Su contable administraba sus inversiones. **The doctor managed to include me in his schedule.** El médico se las arregló para incluirme en su horario.)

MANGA. *Manga* is the term that denotes the width of a boat.

See also *eslora*.

MANGA. *Manga* designa el dibujo animado, o cómic, japonés que trata un tema de aventuras o de ciencia ficción. (**Japanese manga is very popular in the United States.** El cómic japonés es muy popular en los Estados Unidos.)

MANERAS. *Maneras* is translated into English as *ways*. (**Esto puede hacerse de varias maneras.** There are different ways of doing this.)

MANNERS. *Manners* son buenos hábitos, buena educación. (**The young man had good manners.** Era un joven bien educado.)

MARINO. *Marino*, apart from being the adjective that refers to the sea (*mar*), may mean a *sailor*, also called **marinero**. (**Los nudos marinos tienen su belleza especial.** Marine knots have their special beauty. **Eligió ser marino para ver mundo.** He chose to be a sailor to see the world.)

MARINE. Aparte de su uso como adjetivo, **marine** es en Estados Unidos un *infante de marina*, miembro de un sector especializado de las fuerzas armadas. (**The marine environment.** El medio marino. **A platoon of Marines guards the embassy of the United States.** Un destacamento de infantes de marina cuida la embajada de los Estados Unidos.)

MAYOR. *Mayor* means *elder*. (**El hermano mayor os vigila.** Big Brother watches over you.) *Mayor* as a military rank is translated as *major*. (**Un mayor es superior a un teniente.** A major ranks above a lieutenant.)

MAYOR. *The mayor* es el *alcalde*. (**The mayor presides over the municipal council.** El alcalde preside el ayuntamiento.)

MÉDICO. We do not have to elaborate on the meaning of *médico*, *doctor* or *physician*.

MEDIC. *Medic* es aféresis of *paramedic*, el practicante que a falta de médico llevan las ambulancias para prestar primeros auxilios a un accidentado o víctima de un ataque cardíaco por ejemplo. (**The paramedics arrived within minutes of the call.** Los paramédicos llegaron a minutos de la llamada.)

Medio ambiente. The modern Spanish equivalent for *environment*. Before an awareness of the importance of the environment set in, in Spanish it was referred to as *medio* or *ambiente*, making *medio ambiente* a redundant expression. The Spanish Royal Academy Dictionary defines *medio* precisely as *ambiente, conjunto de factores externos que condicionan biológicamente a los seres*.

Aunque, como se dice en la columna de la izquierda, medio ambiente es una tautología, ya que las dos palabras individualmente significan lo mismo, el uso moderno, incluso en el nombre del organismo de las Naciones Unidas encargado de su defensa, *Programa de las Naciones Unidas para el Medio Ambiente*, hace imposible un cambio.

Medios. *Medios* is shorthand for *medios de difusión* (*the press*, *radio*, and *TV*). (**La Oficina de Información se ocupa de los medios.** The Office of Information deals with the media.)

Media. La expresión inglesa *media* se ha tomado del latín y, por ser plural de *medium*, se traduce al español como *medios*. (**The media covers the gossip about movie stars.** En los medios se tratan los chismes sobre las estrellas del cine.)

Memoria, Memorial. *Memoria*, apart from the sense of *memory*, may signify (together with *memorial*), a *notebook* or most likely a *brief*, a *report*, an *essay*. (**Se sometió a la sociedad científica una memoria sobre la evolución.** A paper on evolution was submitted to the scientific society.)

Memorial. *Memorial* es un establecimiento, un monumento o una celebración dedicada a la memoria de alguna persona o de personas. (**A memorial will remember the victims of 9/11 at Ground Zero.** Habrá un monumento en memoria de las víctimas del 11 de setiembre en el sitio conocido como *ground zero*.)

MEMORIAS. *Memorias* is normally used for the literary souvenirs of an author or an era. (**En varios libros de los protagonistas se encontrarán las memorias de la generación del 80.** The memoirs of the members of the generation of the eighties can be found in their different works.)

MEMOIRS, MEMORIES. *Memories* equivale a *reminiscencias*, en tanto que *memoirs* son las memorias literarias o los recuerdos de una vida. (**The memories of the civil war still linger in Spain.** Las reminiscencias de la guerra civil siguen vivas en España. **He wrote his memoirs with the assistance of an editor.** Escribió sus memorias con la ayuda de un redactor.)

METRO. *Metro* is the unit of measurement used in countries that use the metric system. The word is also used as an abbreviation of *metropolitano* to designate the underground transit system (*el metro*). (**El metro de Nueva York ya tiene cien años.** The New York subway is already 100 years old.)

METER, METRO. Aunque no se use el sistema métrico en países de habla inglesa, en Estados Unidos se utiliza la palabra *meter* como medidor. (**The meter for my parked car is about to expire.** Está a punto de caducar la hora del parquímetro de mi coche.) *Metro* se usa a veces para designar las aglomeraciones de grandes ciudades y sus suburbios: *metro New York*, *el Gran Nueva York*.

MILICIA. In Spanish, this term may be ambiguous and refer to an army or an armed group. (**El gobierno organizó una milicia para guardar las fronteras.** The government organized a militia to guard the borders.)

MILITIA. Cuando en inglés se habla de *militia*, se entiende una fuerza armada compuesta de civiles. (**A fierce militia harassed the army.** Una milicia brava hostigó al ejército.)

MINISTRO. *Minister* and ***ministro*** are exact equivalents.

MINISTER. ***To minister*** puede querer decir *administrar, asistir, proveer.* (**The nurse ministered to the sick patient.** La enfermera asistía al enfermo.)

MINUTO, MINUTA. ***Minuto*** is the equivalent of *minute.* ***Minuta*** is a brief record of a meeting, which sometimes just registers the names of those present and the decisions taken. (**La minuta no recogía la dura polémica.** The record did not mention the heated discussion.) ***Minuta*** is also an invoice submitted by a professional, like a lawyer or a notary. (**La minuta estaba calculada según la tabla de honorarios.** The bill was established according to the fee schedule.)

MINUTE. ***Minute*** es el equivalente exacto del *minuto* español. Para referirse a actas, se habla de ***meeting minutes.*** (**To dispel any doubt, they consulted the minutes.** Para disipar toda duda, consultaron las actas.)

MISERABLE. The meaning prevalent in Spanish is that of *vile, wretched, abject.* (**No he conocido a nadie tan miserable.** I never met anyone so wretched.)

MISERABLE. En ambos idiomas *miserable* significa *infeliz.* (**The old man led a miserable existence.** El anciano llevaba una existencia miserable.)

MISERIA. In a figurative sense, it is employed in Spanish to mean very poor circumstances or a very limited amount of money. (**Vivía en la miseria.** He led a life of misery. **Dejó una miseria como propina.** He left a minimal tip.)

MISTERIO. In both languages, these words mean *something secret, unknown or arcane*, but in Spanish the word is also associated with performances of a religious character, generally about the life of Jesus Christ. (**En Semana Santa suelen representarse antiguos misterios.** During the Holy Week, old mystery plays are performed.)

MYSTERY. *Mystery* es una novela de detectives. (**For long plane rides I bring along a mystery to read.** Para largos viajes en avión, me llevo una novela detectivesca.)

MISTIFICAR. *Mistificar* means *to lie, to falsify*. (**El predicador mistificó a la grey sobre el sentido del versículo.** The preacher lied to the congregation about the meaning of the verse.)

MYSTIFY. *To mystify*, se emplea sobre todo en el sentido de *dejar perplejo, confundir, desconcertar*. (**The magician's tricks mystified the public.** El público quedó desconcertado ante los trucos del mago.)

MODERADOR. *Moderador* is one who keeps the center between two extremes. (**Su posición le ayudaba a ser moderador ante los dos partidos.** His position helped him to moderate between the two parties.)

MODERATOR. Término parlamentario, utilizado también en radio y televisión, para designar a una persona considerada imparcial para que dirija una discusión entre posiciones diferentes. (**The round table had a fair moderator.** La mesa redonda tuvo a un moderador imparcial.)

MODESTIA. *Modestia* is *self-effacement, lack of pretense, humility*. (**Aunque muy cultivado, es hombre modesto.** He is a cultivated, but unassuming man.)

MODESTY. Tal vez la acepción más corriente de *modesty* sea *pudor, recato, castidad*. (**Young girls can be more attractive being modest.** Las jóvenes pueden ser más atrayentes siendo recatadas.)

MOLESTAR. In Spanish, this word means *to bother*. (**Le molestó su insistencia.** His insistence bothered her.)

MOLEST, MOLESTATION. En inglés estas palabras se aplican a los casos de *pedofilia*. (**A well-known showman is prosecuted for child molestation.** Un artista bien conocido es juzgado por pedofilia.)

MOMENTÁNEO. Something that is *momentáneo* is *of a very short duration*, or *will happen very soon*. (**Fue una duda momentánea.** He hesitated just for an instant.)

MOMENTOUS, MOMENTARILY. *Momentous* es *trascendental, extraordinario*. (**At the time, women's franchise was a momentous achievement.** En su momento, el voto femenino fue una conquista fundamental.) *Momentarily*, como *momentáneo*, significa *in a short while*. (**The train will begin to move momentarily.** El tren iniciará su marcha dentro de un momento.)

MOMENTO. In Spanish, a *momento* is *a short period of time*. (**Dentro de un momento.** In a moment.)

MOMENTUM. La misma raíz, y un significado diferente en los dos idiomas. En inglés, *momentum* significa *impulso, ímpetu*. (**We have to keep the momentum and continue working.** Debemos mantener el impulso y seguir trabajando.)

MORAL, MORALEJA. *Moral* is *ethics, ethical*, or, like *moraleja*, *the moral of a story*. (**La moraleja del cuento resulta evidente.** The moral of the story is evident.)

MORAL, MORALE. En inglés, *moral* es *ético* o *moraleja*, y *morale* el *estado de ánimo que responde a un impulso exterior*, positivo o negativo. (**Outsourcing and downsizing affected the morale of the staff.** La contratación externa y las reducciones afectaron el ánimo del personal.)

MOROSO. *Deudor moroso* is someone late in a payment due. (**El deudor moroso está sujeto a un cargo de 30 dólares.** Delinquent accounts are subject to a 30 dollar finance charge.)

MOROSE. *Morose* quiere decir *malhumorado, adusto, serio.* (**The sad news left him morose.** La triste noticia lo dejó malhumorado.)

MOTORISTA. DRAE restricts the use of *motorista* to the *driver of a motorcycle.* (**El motorista zigzagueaba entre los coches.** The motorcyclist zigzagged between cars.)

MOTORIST. Un *motorist* es un *automovilista.* (**New York's Central Park drives are closed to motorists.** Las calles que atraviesan el Parque Central de Nueva York están cerradas a los automovilistas.)

MOVER. *Mover* is *to change something from its place,* and also *to advance a piece in chess.* (**Movió el alfil sin pensarlo.** He moved the bishop without thinking about it.)

MOVE. Hay que prestar atención a los casos en que se usa *to move* con el significado de *mudar* o *trasladar.* (**The former neighbor moved to a nicer area.** El antiguo vecino se mudó a una zona mejor. **He moved his books from the study to the living room.** Trasladó los libros del estudio al salón.) *To make a move* significa *mover una pieza, dar un paso* o *recurrir a un método, un procedimiento* enderezado a cierto fin. (**He made the first move towards reconciliation.** Dio el primer paso hacia la reconciliación.)

Ms. There is no equivalent Spanish for this particle, which intends to do away with a different treatment between women of different marital status. *Señora* y *señorita* are the traditional ways in Spain and Latin America for married and unmarried women, although *Señora* is becoming more popular to resolve cases of doubt. In government service, more and more when reporting about someone in the papers, that is the case. The fact that many professional and business women now occupy positions that were in the past denied to them accounts for this. Documents for women are issued and renewed on the maiden name of the bearer. Historically, one can find the treatment *señorita* applied to lower-class servants by their master.

Ms. En los Estados Unidos se adoptó la forma *Ms.* para no diferenciar entre una mujer casada (*Mrs.*) y una soltera (*Miss*). La convención permite evitar la torpeza de dirigirse a alguien con la formula equivocada, aunque normalmente el uso se restringe al texto escrito. *Ms.* se adosa al nombre usual de la persona, sea el nombre de soltera (*maiden name*) o de casada (*married name*). Esto es tanto más común puesto que muchas profesionales y mujeres de negocios ocupan hoy cargos que trradicionalmente fueran reservados a hombres. Esto ha hecho también que ya no se den casos como el identificar a una mujer con el nombre de su marido (*Mrs. John Smith*, y no *Mrs. Mary Smith*, por ejemplo).

MUDA. Apart from its usual meaning, *mute*, **muda** in Spanish may refer to a change of clothes. (**Mi ideal es viajar con sólo una muda de ropa.** It is my ideal to travel with just one change of clothes.)

MUTE. Entre los mandos de la televisión; *mute* quiere decir *con el sonido apagado*. (**During the long series of commercials, I keep the TV on mute.** Durante la larga serie de anuncios, apago el sonido de la televisión.)

MUNICIPAL. *Municipal* refers to a *municipality*, the unit that can comprise a city or a slightly wider district, but certainly the smaller division of the administration in any country. (**La ordenanza municipal imponía fuertes multas a los infractores.** The city order fined violators heavily.) In some countries, *municipal* is a *local policeman*. (**El municipal le impuso una multa.** The local policeman gave him a fine.)

MUNICIPAL. En derecho, además de *derecho propio de un municipio*, *municipal law* significa *legislación interna* o *doméstica*, por oposición a derecho internacional. (**Municipal law cannot contradict national legislation.** El derecho interno no puede contradecir la legislación nacional.)

NAVE. *Nave* as part of a church is translated as *nave*. But in Spanish it also means a *ship* (including a spaceship, *nave espacial*) or a *plane* (also called *aeronave*). (**La nave desplazaba 3.000 toneladas.** The vessel weighed 3,000 tons.) Another meaning of *nave* is an *industrial building*. (**En la zona industrial había inmensas naves.** The industrial area had huge buildings.)

NAVE. *Nave* como *parte central de una iglesia* es la acepción retenida en inglés. (**The nave at Chartres is imposing.** La nave de Chartres es imponente.)

NECESITAR. *Necesitar* is translated as *to need*. (**Necesito dinero.** I need money.)

NECESSITATE. Más que *necesitar*, el sentido de la voz inglesa es *requerir, reclamar*. (**Good salesmanship necessitates good training.** Un buen vendedor requiere buena formación.)

NEGLIGENCIA. The equivalent of *negligencia* is *negligence*. **(Puede acusarse a los padres de negligencia si sus hijos sufren heridas en un accidente por no haber estado atados.** Parents may be accused of negligence if their unsecured children suffer injury in an accident.)

NEGLECT. *Neglect* quiere decir *falta de cuidados* o *desatención*, a menudo culposa o criminal. **(Many cases of neglect of old parents are reported.** Se comunican muchos casos de falta de cuidados a padres ancianos.)

NEGOCIAR. No special remark about the original meanings of these two words.

NEGOTIATE. Un vehículo puede *negotiate* una cuesta, por ejemplo, o sea realizar algo que entraña una cierta dificultad. **(After the snowstorm, the bus had difficulty negotiating the hill.** Tras la tormenta de nieve, al autobús le resultaba difícil salvar la cuesta.)

NEGRO. Spanish has no other word for the list mentioned in the next column; simply *negro*, which has no derogatory form unless other qualifiers are added. Other usual meanings of *negro* include *mercado negro (black market)*, several expressions denoting bad luck (*ánimo negro*), and difficult situations (*vérselas negras*). *See Politically correct.*

NEGRO. La discriminación ha causado la evolucion del tratamiento de la palabra *Negro*, aplicada a una presunta raza de individuos en los Estados Unidos. En otra época se usó el despectivo *nigger*, y se llegó a *colored people* (gente *de color*), para luego preferir *black* y, finalmente, *African-Americans*. La asociación creada para luchar contra la discriminación, *The National Association for the Advancement of Colored People* decidió en 2005 mantener en su nombre la palabra *colored*, tal vez por motivos sentimentales e históricos. Para *African-Americans*, véase el artículo *Politically correct.*

NERVIO. *Nervio* and *nerve* share the same basic meanings. *Nervio* also can signify *great energy, élan.* (**Atacaba el trabajo con gran nervio.** He approached work with great energy.)

NERVE. *To have nerve* es *tener cara, tupé, coraje.* Suele ilustrarse con la historia judía del chico que mata al padre y a la madre y pide que lo consientan como huérfano. (**He had the nerve to deny his actions.** Tuvo cara para negar lo que había hecho.)

NIVEL DE, A. *A nivel de* is a phrase taken from the French *à niveau de* meaning *at the level of* in English. It is as useless there as it is in Spanish. It is an expression in vogue that does not add a thing.

LEVEL OF, AT THE. Si acaso se encontrara la expresión inútil *at the level of* en un texto inglés, cabría reemplazarla por *en cuanto a, con respecto a.*

NOMBRES GEOGRAFICOS.
Geographical names pose several
difficulties for the translator.
Rare names obviously can
be rendered as in the original
(English or Spanish). The present
trend in organizations that deal
with their standardization is to
respect the original, making use
of the approved transliteration
guidelines from the different
source languages. But there are
several other problems: 1) Many
names have been "anglicized" or
"hispanicized" over the years, and
they are normally well-known
and established. 2) Others refer
to disputed places or features (or
their names have been politicized)
and have to be rendered according
to the interests of the author of
the text (Arabian Sea/Persian
Gulf, Malvinas/Falkland, Bay of
Biscay/Golfo de Vizcaya, English
Channel/Canal de la Mancha,
etc.). 3) There are cases of
multiple translations of the same
place (Aachen, Aquisgrán, Aix-
la-Chapelle). 4) The respective
country insists on the name in
the original language, even if it
has been traditionally translated
(Côte d'Ivoire, Timor-Leste).
5) Transliteration systems for non-
Latin script languages may vary: in
English, the city spelled Kharkov is
referred to in Spanish as Járkov.

GEOGRAPHICAL NAMES. Los
nombres geográficos plantean
diferentes problemas al traductor.
Evidentemente, los menos
comunes (trátese de ingleses
o españoles) pueden citarse
en el original. En verdad,
la actual tendencia en las
organizaciones que se ocupan
de su normalización es de
respetar el original, utilizando
las normas de trasliteración para
los distintos idiomas. Pero varias
otras dificultades aparecen: 1) A
través de los años se acuñaron
versiones en inglés o español
respectivamente de muchos
nombres, que han quedado
consagradas definitivamente.
2) Otros se refieren a lugares o
accidentes geográficos en conflicto
o de designaciones politizadas,
y deben respetarse los intereses
del autor del texto (Mar Arábigo/
Golfo Pérsico, Malvinas/Falkland,
Golfo de Vizcaya/Bay of Biscay,
English Channel/Canal de la
Mancha, etc.). 3) Hay casos de
nombres múltiples para un mismo
lugar, como Aachen, Aquisgrán
y Aix-la-Chapelle. 4) El país de
que se trata insiste en que se dé
el nombre en el idioma original,
aun cuando anteriormente se haya
conocido siempre con el traducido
(Côte d'Ivoire, Timor-Leste).
5) Los sistemas de trasliteración
de lenguas en caracteres latinos
difieren según los países: la ciudad
que en inglés se escribe Kharkov
se vuelve Jarkov en español.

NOTICIA, NUEVAS. *Noticia, nuevas*, or *novedades* are translated as *news*. (**Que no haya noticias es buena noticia.** No news is good news.)

NOTICE, NEWS. *News* es *noticia* (a pesar de la *s*, es un sustantivo singular). (**Today, the news from the political scene is encouraging.** Hoy, las noticias de la escena politica son alentadoras.) *Notice* es *anuncio, advertencia.* (**There is a notice board for announcements, sales and items of interest to the staff.** Hay una cartelera para anuncios, ventas y cuestiones de interés del personal. **Until further notice.** Hasta nuevo aviso.) *To notice* es *observar.* (**The plainclothesman was unnoticed.** El policía de paisano pasó inadvertido.)

NUDO. *Nudo* can be several things: *A marine knot* is a measure of speed, the unit being a mile in an hour. (**El barco avanzaba a 20 nudos.** The boat made 20 knots.) It can be a railway, airline, or communications *hub*, in general; a simple *knot*; *nudo* in the sense of *desnuda*, a legal term as applied to property means *title but no right of use* (**sin usufructo**, according to DRAE).

NUDE. Un *desnudo artístico* es un *nude*. (**He painted his model in the nude.** Pintó un desnudo de su modelo. **She inherited the nude property of the house.** Heredó la nuda propiedad.)

OBLIGAR. *Obligar* is normally translated as *to force, to compel.* (**La obligó a seguirlo.** He forced her to follow him.)

OBLIGE. *To oblige* es también *agradecer, complacer, retribuir, reciprocar.* (**I asked him to find out something and he obliged.** Le pedí que averiguara algo, y me complació.)

OBSEQUIOSO. *Obsequioso*, according to DRAE, is *"courteous and ready to do what others wish."* (**De carácter obsequioso, podías pedirle cualquier favor.** He was so obliging that you could ask him to render any service.)

OBSEQUIOUS. *Obsequious* significa *dócil, sumiso*, muy cerca de *obsecuente*. (**He was obsequious with his boss to the point of running small errands unrelated to his job.** Era sumiso con su jefe, hasta el punto de hacer mandados que nada tenían que ver con su trabajo.)

OCULTO. *Oculto* is rendered as *hidden*, not *occult*. (**La clave de la caja de caudales estaba bien oculta.** The combination to the safe was well hidden.)

OCCULT. Lo más frecuente es encontrar la palabra *occult* en el sentido de *esotérico, sobrenatural, misterioso*, e incluso como sustantivo por *ocultismo*. (**He studied the occult in different religions.** Estudió lo esotérico en diversas religiones.)

OCURRENCIA. *Ocurrencia* is *a funny idea, a witty remark*. (**Una ocurrencia graciosa hace soportable un largo discurso.** A witty remark makes a long speech bearable.)

OCCURRENCE. *Occurrence* deriva de ocurrir, y significa *acaecimiento*. (**In his research, he noted the occurrence of a certain event over time.** Para su investigación, tomó nota de las veces que se presentaba cierto hecho en el tiempo.)

OFENSA. See *Injury*.

OFFENCE. En el catálogo de faltas contra derecho, una *offence* es una *contravención*. (**There is an established fine for that offence.** Hay una multa fija para esa contravención.)

OFICIAL. *Oficial* in Spanish is something *authoritative* or named as truly representative. (**El responsable oficial de los museos es el Ministerio de Cultura.** The authority in charge of museums is the Ministry of Culture.)

OFFICER, OFFICIAL. En el caso de un agente de policía o de un oficial de las fuerzas armadas, se dice *officer*, para un burócrata o administrativo se emplea la palabra *official*; en ambos casos se traduce al español por la palabra *oficial*, que también se aplica al trabajador manual avezado. (**He was stopped by an officer at the crossroads.** Un oficial lo hizo detener en el cruce. **The official in charge approved his application.** El funcionario competente aprobó su solicitud. **Some enterprises became official sponsors of the Expo.** Algunas firmas comerciales se hicieron patrocinadoras de la Expo.) Vimos ya que por lo que respecta a documentos, acuerdos, etc., *official* y *unofficial* (informal) son sinónimos de *oficial* y *oficioso*.

OFICIOSO. The first meaning noted in the right-hand column is also true of Spanish: *he who strives to please*. (**Se mostró oficioso en indicarnos las comodidades del lugar.** He officiously showed us all the amenities of the place.)

OFFICIOUS. Esta palabra inglesa puede significar a la vez *amable*, *servicial* o *entrometido*. (**An officious young boy ready to go the extra mile.** Un joven servicial dispuesto a hacer un esfuerzo adicional. **When people talked about their business, he officiously interrupted.** Mientras la gente hablaba de sus cosas, él se entrometía a interrumpir.)

OMBUDSMAN. This word refers to a Scandinavian institution, which combines functions of mediator and of peacemaker. Normally it is not an arbitrator, and cannot impose solutions or be a referee, but is able to clear the air in a conflict; the proceedings do not require naming the adversaries. The terms of reference vary according to the organization where it is established, and given its peculiarity it is better to keep the name untranslated, not even changing the ending *-man* to *-person*.

OMBUDSMAN. Esta es una institución escandinava, que reúne las condiciones del mediador o defensor del pueblo (voces con las que suele traducirse al español) y conciliador. Claro que según la organización en que funcione, sus facultades y modus operandi variarán, pero por lo general, caso Naciones Unidas, respetan el anonimato y no tienen poder de decisión o imposición de sus conclusiones. Por eso es preferible mantener la palabra original sin alterar siquiera el *-man* sexista con el sufijo *-person*.

ÓMNIBUS. *Ómnibus* or *autobús* is the equivalent of *bus*. (**El ómnibus se detiene cada tres calles.** The bus stops every three streets.)

OMNIBUS. El calificativo inglés *omnibus* significa *general*, *colectivo*, que abarca muchos elementos. (**Parliament approved an omnibus law on the budget.** El Parlamento aprobó una ley general sobre el presupuesto.)

OPERADOR. *Operador* in Spanish is virtually a thing of the past, denoting a person who works at a telephone switchboard, although it also applies to someone who projects a film in a movie theater. (**En otra época había que recurrir a la operadora para hablar a larga distancia.** Some time ago you had to ask the operator to connect you with long distance.)

OPERATOR. Puede tratarse de un telefonista (*telephone operator*), de quien acciona un mecanismo o aparato (*movie house operator*) o del conductor o titular de una licencia de explotación (*bus operator*, *utility operator*).

OPERAR, OPERARSE. While *operar* may be translated as *to operate*, *operarse* is normally rendered as *to undergo surgery*. (**Tuvo que operarse de los riñones.** He had to undergo kidney surgery.)

OPERATE. El verbo inglés suele usarse como transitivo (*operate a vehicle*) en el sentido de *conducir, manejar,* y también *obrar, hacerse cargo de, marchar, surtir efecto.* (**The new system operates perfectly.** El nuevo sistema surte buen efecto.)

OPINIÓN. Has the same meaning as the English word *opinion.*

OPINIONATED. *Opinionated* es la persona de juicios u opiniones muy enraizadas, aunque no necesariamente correctas o meditadas, *testaruda* e *intolerante.* (**She is opinionated, even if facts prove her wrong.** Es testaruda en sus opiniones, aunque los hechos la desvirtúen.)

OPORTUNIDAD, OPORTUNO. In Spanish, *oportuno* means *convenient, timely.* (**Un recordatorio oportuno.** A timely reminder.)

OPPORTUNITY. *Opportunity* y *occasion* son sinónimos. (**It was a favorable opportunity for discussion.** La oportunidad era buena para discutir.)

OPUESTO. *Opuesto* and *opposite* share the same meaning, but as the participle of *oponer*, the former gives the idea of opposition. (**El partido gobernante se mostró opuesto al aborto.** The ruling party stated opposition to abortion.)

OPPOSITE. *Opposite* es lo situado enfrente. (**The house opposite the court.** La casa frente al tribunal.) También, lo contrario u opuesto. (**The opposite of good is bad.** Lo contrario de lo bueno es lo malo.)

ORDENANZA. In Spanish, *ordenanza* is *a decree by a municipal authority*, as well as a military assistant or an orderly at a bureaucratic office. (**Una ordenanza municipal determina la altura máxima de los edificios.** A city regulation determines the maximum height of buildings. **El ordenanza del coronel cumplía para él muchas tareas domésticas.** The colonel's assistant orderly did many house tasks for him.)

ORDNANCE, ORDENANCE, ORDERLY. En inglés, *ordnance* son *municiones* o *pertrechos*, por lo general que no han explotado; *ordenance* corresponde al español *ordenanza*; *orderly*, además del ordenanza militar, o del ayudante enfermero, quiere decir *ordenado*. (**Sites of old conflict have buried unexploded ordnance.** Los lugares donde hubo conflicto tienen aún enterradas municiones sin explotar. **He keeps his papers in an orderly fashion.** Tiene sus papeles bien ordenados.)

ORDINARIO. *Ordinario* means *normal, regular*. (**Presupuesto ordinario.** The regular budget.) But *ordinario* may be equivalent to *basto*, *vulgar*. (**A pesar de su fortuna, tenía gestos ordinarios.** In spite of his wealth, he had vulgar manners.)

ORDINARY. Nada especial que señalar.

PAQUETE. *Paquete* is sometimes used in parliamentary language as the rendering of *package*, a combination of elements or decisions that constitutes a whole that has to be accepted or refused. (**Para resolver el punto muerto propusieron un paquete.** In order to break the deadlock, they submitted a package.)

PACKAGE, PACKET. En un sentido figurado, *packet* significa *fortuna* o *gran suma de dinero* (uso inglés). (**In his attaché case he carried a packet of money.** En su portafolio llevaba una gran suma de dinero.) Antes de los progresos en comunicaciones se usaba para un *paquebote* o *buque correo*. (**The packet ran aground.** El paquebote encalló.) *Package deal* es un arreglo o solución global. (**The budget for the wedding was a package deal, just one figure for all the services.** El presupuesto de la boda se cotizó globalmente, con una sola cifra para todo.)

PARCELA. A *parcela* is a *plot*, a subdivision of land. (**En una pequeña parcela cultivaba un huerto.** He cultivated an orchard on a small plot of land.)

PARCEL. *Parcel* quiere decir *paquete*. (**I sent the books by parcel post.** Envié los libros por encomienda postal.) La expresión *part and parcel* se traduce por *parte integrante, elemento esencial*. (**Music appreciation is part and parcel of a good education.** El gusto por la música es parte integral de una buena educación.)

PARCIALIDAD. *Parcialidad* in Spanish denotes *being partial*. (**Un árbitro no debe mostrar parcialidad.** A referee should not be partial.)

PARTIALITY. *Partiality*, como sinónimo de *bias*, significa *prejuicio*, aunque también puede tener una acepción más neutral: *preferencia, predilección, inclinación*. (**The teacher showed partiality to the foreign student.** El profesor mostraba preferencia por el estudiante extranjero.)

PARIENTES. All members of the extended family are called *parientes*. (**Muchos parientes asistieron a los funerales del finado.** Many relatives attended the service for the deceased.)

PARENTS. No cualquier pariente (término genérico que en español equivale a *relative*), sino los *padres*. (**Parents are legally responsible for their children's actions.** Los padres son jurídicamente responsables por las acciones de sus hijos.)

PARROQUIAL. *Parroquial* is from the *parroquia*, the *parish*, a small territory with a priest in charge of a church and the affairs of the church. (**El cura parroquial venía de otra provincia.** The parish priest came from another province.)

PAROCHIAL. *Parochial* es *parroquial*, aplicado a una escuela católica por ejemplo. Además, igual que *provincial*, define un espíritu estrecho, o una manera de ver las cosas con una óptica de grupo limitado. (**I found the leaders of the conservative party to have a very parochial view of the world.** Comprobé que los dirigentes del partido conservador tenían una visión muy estrecha del mundo.)

PARTICULAR. *Particular* means *private*. In the registration of cars, *particular* stands for *privately owned*, not a company or an official car. (**Cuando estaba de vacaciones conducía su coche particular y no el oficial.** While on holidays he drove his private car, not the official one.)

PARTICULAR. En inglés, *particular* también quiere decir *quisquilloso*, *meticuloso*, *extravagante*. (**He was very particular about his appearance and always wore a suit.** Era muy meticuloso en cuanto a su aspecto y siempre vestía traje.) También puede decirse de un asunto dado. (**Let's talk about that particular.** Hablemos de ese asunto.)

PASIÓN. Normally, no difference in usage of both terms.

PASSION. En inglés a menudo denota *ira, cólera, furor*. (**My friend spoke in a fit of passion about the incident.** Mi amigo habló con ira del incidente.)

PATROCINAR. *Patrocinar* means *to sponsor*. (**Los Juegos Olímpicos fueron patrocinados por grandes firmas.** The Olympic Games were sponsored by big companies.)

PATRONIZE. *Patronize* deriva de *patron* y por eso significa *ser cliente, parroquiano* de un comercio. (**Living in a small village, he tried to patronize the local businesses.** Como vivía en un pueblo pequeño, trataba de ser cliente del comercio local.) También significa *ser condescendiente*, adoptar un aire protector, de paternalismo. (**Don't patronize me, I can fend for myself.** No me trate con paternalismo, puedo defenderme solo.)

PATRÓN, PATRONO. *Patrón* is the *boss*; also the *skipper* or *captain* of a boat; *Santo patrono*, in the Catholic church, is a saint under whose protection a church or a town is placed. (**El patrón del barco dirigía la maniobra.** The skipper conducted the maneuver.)

PATRON. *Patron* es un *cliente*, un *parroquiano*. (**The use of toilets is reserved for patrons.** El uso de los aseos está reservado a los clientes.) *Patron of the arts* es el equivalente inglés de *mecenas*.

PAVIMENTO. In Spanish, *pavimento*, is the *paved road*, as distinct from the *pavement* (UK) or *sidewalk* (US). (**Cuando no hay acera, hay que marchar por el pavimento de frente a los vehículos.** Where there is no sidewalk, you have to walk on the road facing the traffic.)

PAVEMENT. Para un inglés, *pavement* es lo que para el estadounidense es *sidewalk* (*acera*, o *vereda*, en algún país de América hispana). (**You have to look both ways before stepping off the pavement into the road.** Hay que mirar a ambos lados antes de bajar de la acera a la calle.)

PEDESTRE. These words mean basically the same, but *pedestre* is also synonymous with *vulgar*. (**Es conocido por sus comentarios pedestres.** He is known for his vulgar remarks. **Para la fiesta mayor, organizaron una carrera pedestre.** A running contest was organized for the patron saint's fair.)

PEDESTRIAN. Etimológicamente, quiere decir *el que marcha a pie*. (**At street crossings, cars have to yield to pedestrians.** En las intersecciones, los coches deben ceder el paso a los peatones.) También indica algo *ordinario*, sin sutileza. (**The essays are pedestrian, almost vulgar.** Los escritos eran pedestres, casi vulgares.)

PENA. The Spanish word *pena* may be rendered as *sorrow*, *pity*. (**Pena por el fracaso de la obra.** Pity for the failure of the play.)

PAIN. *Pain* quiere decir *dolor*. (**The sick man was in great pain.** El enfermo sentía un gran dolor.)

PERDÓN. The Spanish word *perdón* is usually translated as *forgiveness*. The expression *no perdonar* means to avail oneself of an opportunity to do something convenient. (**No perdonó la oportunidad de ver a su artista favorita.** She would not miss the opportunity to see her favorite artist.)

PARDON. *Pardon*, como término jurídico, se traduce al español como *indulto* (de una pena) o *condonación* (de una deuda). (**The President gives pardons on national holidays.** El Presidente indulta en fiestas nacionales. **Debt from developing countries affected by the tsunami was pardoned.** Se condonó la deuda de países en desarrollo afectados por el tsunami.)

PERSONA. The normal meaning in Spanish is equivalent to *person*.

PERSONA. Se ha dado muy recientemente en hablar de *persona* como la idiosincrasia, las singularidades de un individuo. (**The play focused on the persona of the protagonists rather than on their actions.** La obra se detiene en la idiosincrasia de los protagonistas y no en lo que hacen.)

PERSONAL. The Spanish word *personal* has two meanings: *own* or *staff*. (**La empresa se fundó con mi dinero personal, pero considero que he formado un buen capital en su personal.** I founded the company with my own money, but I believe I have accrued a considerable capital in its personnel.)

PERSONAL, PERSONNEL. En inglés, *personal* es el adjetivo que significa *particular*, *privado*. Para referirnos a la dotación de empleados de una empresa se usa *personnel*, hoy reemplazado a menudo por la expresión *human resources* (*recursos humanos)* como signo de cambio en la filosofía del empleo.

PERSPECTIVA. In Spanish, the ideas of *perspective* and *prospective* are expressed with the term **perspectiva**.

PERSPECTIVE, PROSPECTIVE. Como concepto geométrico, arquitectónico o económico y como sinónimo de *punto de vista*, se usa *perspective*. *Prospective* es lo que se espera lograr. (**Growth in the last three years' perspective has been consistent.** En la perspectiva de los últimos tres años, el crecimiento ha sido consecuente. **For 2006, there will be 10% fewer prospective home buyers.** En 2006, se espera que los adquirentes de casas se reduzcan en un 10%.)

PETULANCIA, PETULANTE. These two words have evolved differently from their root. In Spanish, *petulancia* means *arrogance, haughtiness*. (**La petulancia de ese individuo no correspondía a sus pocas luces.** His arrogance did not go well with his poor intelligence.)

PETULANCE, PETULANT. *Petulance* significa *malhumor, mal genio*. (**His petulance was a barrier to friendship.** Su mal genio era una barrera a la amistad.)

PILOTO. A *piloto* handles the controls of an aircraft. Certain port authorities require the services of a *piloto* or *práctico* when a boat enters the port.

PILOT. *Pilot projects* son *planes experimentales*, prototipos de programas. (**Many internationally funded pilot projects helped nations to start new industries.** Muchos planes experimentales ayudaron a países a iniciar industrias nuevas.)

PLAUSIBLE. In Spanish, the usual meaning of *plausible* is something *commendable, laudable, deserving applause*. (**La organización realiza una obra plausible.** The organization does commendable work.) Recently, DRAE added the sense of *reasonable*.

PLAUSIBLE. En inglés, *plausible* denota algo *razonable, posible*. (**He had a plausible explanation for his delay.** Tuvo una explicación verosímil para su demora.)

POLÍTICA. Mention could be made of derogatory words derived from *política. Politico, politiquero* and *politicastro (politico, petty politician)* are in that category. (**A falta de profesión, se hizo politiquero.** For want of a profession, he became a politico.) Also *politiquear*, an equivalent of *politicking*. (**En lugar de dictar leyes, se dedicaron a politiquear.** Instead of making laws, they were politicking.)

POLICY, POLITICS. *Policy* es una *política, norma, conducta* determinada. (**The store has a return policy.** La tienda tiene reglas para casos de devoluciones.) *Politics* es *la política* como actividad. (**He engaged in politics.** Se dedicó a la política.)

POLÍTICAMENTE CORRECTO.
The phenomenon of political
correctness, typically American,
gained acceptance in Spanish-
speaking countries, where certain
euphemisms were already widely
used. *No vidente* replaced *ciego*
(*blind*), nobody spoke any more
of *tullido* but *discapacitado*
(*handicapped*). Also, for titles or
professions the masculine noun
was normally used: *Embajador,*
médico could be applied to
women. Not any more: even nouns
derived from present participles are
"feminized" like *Presidenta*, where
Presidente was right for both
genders, Even words like *jueza*
are created to design a female
magistrate. And there are words
considered to be very incorrect like
invertido for *homosexual* or *gay*.

See **Género.**

POLITICALLY CORRECT. En los
Estados Unidos hubo enormes
progresos en la lucha contra
la discriminación, tanto étnica
como contra la mujer, por
edad, religión, etc. Esto llevó
a una revisión de términos que
se juzgaban peyorativos o tan
sólo característicos de épocas
pasadas, en general machistas.
Las nuevas denominaciones
resultantes fueron en algunos casos
innovadoras, en otros eufemismos
y algunas sencillamente tonterías.
Un caso especial es el de las
denominaciones de profesiones
o títulos. *Cartero*, un sustantivo
masculino, no puede designar
a una mujer; es *letter carrier* o
postal worker, nunca *mailman.*
Policía será *police officer.* El
presidente de un comité es
chairperson, a veces *chairwoman,*
y hasta *chair.* Se habla de *sexual*
orientation y no de *homosexuality.*
(La abreviatura *GLTB* designa
al colectivo *gays, lesbianas,*
transexuales y *bisexuales.*)

Véase el artículo Género.

PORTERO. *Portero* is *one who*
guards a door (*puerta*, in
Spanish), and also the *goalkeeper*
in football (*arquero* in Latin
America). (**El nuevo portero**
detuvo un penalti. The new goalkeeper stopped a penalty kick.)

PORTER. *Porter* es el *mozo de*
cordel o *cargador.* (**The trolleys**
at airports mean less work
for porters. Los carritos de
aeropuertos hacen que tengan
menos trabajo los cargadores.)

POSICIÓN. *Posición* and *position* have equivalent meanings. In some cases it may be better to translate the Spanish word as *ranking*. (**Su posición en tenis es destacada.** His ranking in tennis is very high.)

POSITION, SITUATION. *Position* y *situation* parecen palabras intercambiables por lo que se refiere al estado de las finanzas o de las cuentas de una persona. (**His account's position was quite comfortable.** La situación de su cuenta era bastante desahogada.) *Position* puede ser también *cargo, puesto.* (**Good positions require adequate training.** Los buenos cargos exigen una capacitación apropiada.)

PRÁCTICO, PRÁCTICA. *Práctico* is equivalent to *practical*, as the opposite of theoretical. It is also the name given to the local pilot required of a boat that enters a port, because of under-currents, dredging, etc. (**Las autoridades portuarias de Buenos Aires exigen un práctico para la operación de atraque.** The port authorities of Buenos Aires require a local pilot for docking.) *Práctica* is opposed, or complementary, to *teoría* (*theory*). (**Sabe mucha teoría, pero le falta práctica.** He knows the theory, but lacks in practice.)

PRACTICAL, PRACTICE. En inglés, la *practice* de un médico es su consultorio y sus pacientes. (**The doctor started a practice in a poor neighborhood.** El médico instaló su consultorio en un barrio pobre.)

PRACTICANTE. *Practicante* is the *practitioner* of a science or a technique, or one who practices a religion. (**Como judío practicante, no trabaja el sábado.** Being a practicing Jew, he does not work on the Sabbath.) *Practicante* is the advanced medical student who gives basic care to sick people. *See Medic.*

PRACTITIONER, PRACTICING. Es *practitioner* el que se dedica a un arte o una técnica. (**Practitioners of homeopathics have to convince patients that their method works.** Los adeptos de la homeopatía deben convencer a los pacientes de que su método es eficaz.)

PRECINTO. A *precinto* is a *strap* used to close access to a site under legal or administrative investigation or a means of securing a suitcase, a *luggage strap.* (**Se cerró con precinto la entrada al restaurante cerrado por violaciones al código de higiene.** The access to the restaurant closed for violations to the hygiene code was sealed with a strap.)

PRECINCT. En los Estados Unidos, *precinct* es *una comisaría policial de barrio.* (**The precinct in the Puerto Rican neighborhood has officers who speak Spanish fluently.** La comisaría situada en el barrio puertorriqueño cuenta con agentes que hablan un español corriente.)

PRECIOSO. Colloquially, *precioso* means *pretty, very nice.* (**La niña es preciosa.** The girl is very pretty.)

PRECIOUS. Los significados de ambas voces son prácticamente identicos. En inglés, *precious* supone también algo muy especial.

PRECISAR. *Precisar* means *to need.* (**Se precisa más personal para aumentar la producción.** In order to increase production, additional personnel are needed.)

PRECISE.

PREDICAMENTO. Here, the meanings diverge in a curious way. The Spanish word means *repute, influence, dignity*. (**El candidato goza de gran predicamento en su distrito.** The candidate is a man of great repute in his district.)

PREDICAMENT. *Predicament* es muy diferente de *predicamento*. Significa *tribulación, apuro, dificultad*. (**The inhabitants of the flooded city were in a terrible predicament.** Los pobladores de la ciudad inundada pasaban por grandes apuros.)

PREMISAS. *Premisa* is a point of departure, a *hypothesis*. (**La premisa es que no habrá guerra.** The assumption is that there will be no war.) *For Premise, see Scenario.*

PREMISES. *Made on the premises* significa hecho en el mismo lugar, no fuera de él. (**There is a sign in the bakery saying that cakes are made on the premises.** En la panadería hay un cartel que dice que las tortas se preparan en el lugar.)

PRE-OWNED, PRE-VIEWED. Quiero incluir aquí una de las curiosas manías estadounidenses de dar nombres pretenciosos a cosas simples. Un coche *previously owned* o *pre-owned*, o un *pre-viewed DVD* no son otra cosa que artículos *usados* o *de segunda mano*; tímidamente se ha pretendido alejarse del aparentemente vejatorio *usado*.

PREPARACIÓN. In Spanish, *preparación* may mean *medicines*, what used to be called *fórmula magistral*, with ingredients mixed by the chemist. (**El farmacéutico había formulado una preparación muy eficaz contra el estreñimiento.** The pharmacist had made a preparation which treated constipation effectively.)

PREPARATION.

PRESCRIPCIÓN. *Prescripción* is a general term for a *directive*, a norm to be followed (**En tráfico, deben observarse prescripciones claras.** Clear rules are required for traffic regulation.), and also for what in common law (*derecho tradicional*) is known as the *statute of limitations*, the period after which a right or a penalty ceases to be exercisable. (**La multa ha prescrito a los dos años.** According to the statute of limitations, after two years' time the fine can no longer be demanded.)

PRESCRIPTION. *Prescription* quiere decir *receta*, incluso en sentido figurado. (**He gave him a prescription for his illness.** Le dio una receta para su mal. **Moderation at the table and daily exercise are a prescription for good health.** La moderación en la mesa y el ejercicio diario son una receta para la buena salud.)

PRESENTE, PRESENTAR. Speaking of a person, *presentar* means *to introduce*. *Presente* is a *gift*, and there are other meanings of *presentar* common to both languages.

PRESENT. Se dice *to present someone with a prize* (*entregarle un premio*). (**The Mayor presented him with a certificate of merit.** El alcalde le otorgó un certificado al mérito.)

PRESERVAR. *Preservar* means *to protect, to guard.* (**Se ha preservado el carácter no comercial de la emisora oficial.** The non-commercial character of State broadcasting has been preserved.)

PRESERVE. Además de *resguardar* y *proteger*, acepciones que también tiene *preservar* en español, significa *conservar*. (**The buildings in that village were preserved as they were at the time of the wars of independence.** Los edificios de esa aldea se conservan como eran en tiempos de la guerra de la independencia.) Como sustantivo, *preserve* significa *propiedad exclusiva* o *confitura*. (**The national park is the preserve of its animals.** El parque nacional es el dominio exclusivo de sus animales. *Peach preserves, confitura de melocotones*)

PRESS. *Press* es una palabra de acepciones múltiples, entre ellas *apremiar, obligar, planchar, persuadir, recalcar, importunar* y claro, *prensar*. Como sustantivo, está *presión, prensa,* e *imprenta.* (**The Press has been called the fourth power.** A la prensa se la llama el cuarto poder.)

PRESUMIR. *Presumir* means *to boast*, to have a high opinion of oneself. (***Presumía de adonis.*** He considered himself an Adonis.)

PRESUME. *To presume* se traduce de ordinario por *suponer, dar por sentado*. (**Mr. Holmes, I presume?** Supongo que usted es el Sr. Holmes.)

PRETENDER. The Spanish term means *to aspire*, and is also used with a more specific meaning, *to court*. (**Pretendía llegar a la universidad.** He aspired to go to college. **Pretendía a la vecina.** He was courting his neighbor.)

PRETEND. *To pretend* significa *aparentar, fingir, simular.* (**The patient pretended to have been injured by his boss.** El paciente simuló haber sido herido por su patrón.)

PRETENSIÓN. In Spanish, *pretensión* implies the idea of wanting to be considered as something one is not. (**Tenía la pretensión de considerarse experto en vinos.** He fancied himself an expert on wine.)

PRETENCE. *Pretence* quiere decir *jactancia, vanagloria* y también *fingimiento, apariencia engañosa.* (**There was a pretence of art in that awful sculpture.** Se buscaba una apariencia de arte en esa horrible escultura.)

PREVENIR, PREVER. *Prevenir* originally meant *to foresee, to see in advance.* (**Parece que pudo prevenirse el reciente tsunami.** It looks like the recent tsunami could have been foreseen.) It includes the element of doing something to take care of the problem. *Prever* is *to forecast, to conjecture.* (**Se prevé una buena cosecha.** A good harvest is forecast.)

PREVENT. *To prevent* suele tener hoy una connotación negativa, *obstruir, impedir.* (**Any union job action has to be prevented.** Hay que impedir toda acción de reivindicación del sindicato.)

PRIVADO. *Reunión en privado* is a *closed meeting.* (**Antes de la conferencia de prensa, se reunieron en privado.** Before the press conference, they had a closed meeting.)

PRIVATE. *Private* es el primer grado de un suboficial en el ejército estadounidense, lo que sería un *cabo* en otros. *Private car* es un automóvil particular.

PROACTIVO. This word is almost never used in its true sense. What it actually means in conference procedure is simply *a dialogue*, a discussion that allows an informal exchange, with questions and answers, comments and reviews. The reality is that debates normally become a series of isolated speeches.

PROACTIVE. *Proactive* o *interactive* ha pasado a ser una palabra preferida en los ambientes de la ONU, donde pretende referirse a un *diálogo* (plática entre dos o más personas, según el DRAE), un debate no estructurado, con intervenciones de preguntas, respuestas y comentarios espontáneos, cosa que casi nunca ocurre.

PROBAR. The translation of *probar* is *to prove*. (**Los hechos probaron que tenía razón.** Facts proved me right.)

PROBE, PROVE. *Probe* es una *sonda*. De ahí *to probe*, *sondear*, *indagar*. (**The government ordered a probe into a case of corruption.** El gobierno ordenó una indagación en un caso de corrupción.)

PROCEDIMIENTO. *Procedimiento*, besides *procedure*, means in legal terms *a judicial or administrative action*. (**La policía realizó un procedimiento en un lugar bajo sospecha de ser un refugio de delincuentes.** The police went to a place suspected of being a safe house for criminals.)

PROCEDURE. *Procedure* es un sinónimo perfecto de *procedimiento*.

PROCESO. The two words are equivalent in their original meanings.

PROCESS. También en este caso, un barbarismo, *process*, por *elaborar*, se ha infiltrado en el uso diario, por ejemplo en *EDP, electronic data processing* (*elaboración electrónica de datos*) o para *tramitar*, en el caso de una solicitud, por ejemplo. (**It takes a couple of days to process a visa.** Lleva un par de días tramitar el visado.)

PROCURA, PROCURACIÓN. *En procura de* means *in search of*. *Procuración* is a *proxy, power of attorney*, or *delegation of authority*. (**Viajó a España en procura de empleo.** He traveled to Spain in search of a job. **Dio procuración a su hermano.** She gave power of attorney to her brother.)

PROCUREMENT. *Procurement* no es ni búsqueda ni nada parecido, sino *compra, adquisición*. (**Government procurement is subject to strict rules of bidding, accountability, and audits.** Las adquisiciones del gobierno están sometidas a reglas estrictas de licitación, rendición de cuentas y auditoría.)

PROCURAR. *Procurar* and *procure*, with the exception noted in the right-hand column, are synonymous.

PROCURE, PROCURER. *To procure*, además de su significado de *conseguir*, significa *alcahuetear*. (**In his police file, he had several entries as a procurer.** En su prontuario policial, había varios ingresos por alcahuetería.)

PRODUCTO. *Producto*, like *article*, is a general term for *goods*. It is also used in both languages for some economic/statistical terms such as *producto nacional bruto* (*GDP, gross domestic product*), etc.

PRODUCE, PRODUCT. El uso hace de *produce* una categoría especial de productos: *frutos y legumbres*. **(Produce in the United States may have to travel long distances to the markets.** En los Estados Unidos las frutas y legumbres deben recorrer largas distancias hasta llegar a los mercados.)

PROGRESO. There are no special remarks about usage of the Spanish word *progreso*, always used with a clear meaning.

PROGRESS. *Progress* puede no significar *progreso* concreto sino el avance hacia un objetivo. **(You can follow on screen the progress of surgery.** Se puede seguir en la pantalla la marcha de una operación quirúrgica.) *A progress report* es un informe sobre la marcha de los trabajos. *A meeting in progress*, una reunión ya iniciada, en marcha.

PROPAGANDA. In Latin America particularly, *propaganda* is also used in the sense of *publicity*, *advertisement*. **(La propaganda comercial en televisión excede los límites de lo razonable.** Advertising on TV goes beyond all reasonable bounds.)

PROPAGANDA. La palabra inglesa significa ideas, hechos o alegatos difundidos deliberadamene para promover una causa o despresitigiar la del opositor. (*In times of war, the combatants' propaganda often uses lies or half-truths.* En épocas de guerra, la propaganda de los beligerantes se sirve de mentiras o de verdades a medias.)

PROPIEDAD. All of the English terms listed in the right column are rendered in Spanish by ***propiedad***.

PROPERTY, PROPRIETY, PROPRIETARY. He aquí varias palabras inglesas con muy distinto significado: ***property*** es *propiedad*; ***propriety*** es *corrección*; ***proprietary***, que se aplicaba a los derechos absolutos de propiedad en una colonia, antiguamente, hoy se reserva a las *medicinas patentadas*, o sea, con un derecho de *propiedad industrial* o *intelectual*. (**He treated the subordinates with delicate propriety.** Trató a sus subordinados con fina corrección. **Proprietary medicines are replaced in time by generics.** Los medicamentos patentados se reemplazan al cabo del tiempo por genéricos.)

PROPIO. The two words share the meanings of *distinctive*, *appropriate,* and *right* or *correct*. But in Spanish there are other concepts: *normal*, *own*. (**Lo propio es hablar sinceramente.** It is normal to speak sincerely. **Pagó los gastos de su propio peculio.** He paid the expenses out of his own pocket.) There is also the archaic meaning—little used—of *emissary, messenger*. (**Envió a un propio con un mensaje urgente.** He sent an emissary with an urgent message.)

PROPER. Lo más común es utilizar ***proper*** como *correcto, formal*. (**Not only is he very proper dealing with customers, but he often solves their problems immediately.** No sólo trata muy formalmente a los clientes, sino que a menudo resuelve de inmediato sus problemas.)

PROPONER. In Spanish, it is common to use this verb in the pronominal form, meaning *to intend*. (**Se propuso caminar tres kilómetros cada día.** He intended to walk three kilometres a day.)

PROPOSE. *To propose* también quiere decir *declararse, pedir la mano*. (**After long hesitation, Max proposed to Rachel.** Tras largas vacilaciones, Max pidió la mano de Raquel.)

PROPOSICIÓN, PROPUESTA. A *propuesta* is a *proposal* submitted to an authority or legislative body for a decision to be made. (**El Consejo Escolar envió una propuesta de comedor escolar al Ayuntamiento.** The Education Council submitted a proposal on a school cafeteria to City Hall. **Su propuesta de matrimonio no cayó bien.** His marriage proposal did not fall on good ears.)

PROPOSAL, PROPOSITION. *Proposition* puede traducirse a veces por *tesis, afirmación, proyecto*. Otros sentidos de la palabra son: el pedido de una relación sexual o una tesis (matemática, por ejemplo) para el debate. (**He made a direct proposition to her.** La invitó directamente a acostarse con él. **The teacher demonstrated the proposition to the class.** El profesor hizo una demostración de la tesis ante los alumnos.)

PROSODIA. In Spanish, *prosodia* is the series of norms regarding intonation and accent. (**La prosodia del chino es de naturaleza muy diferente.** The Chinese norms on accent are quite different.)

PROSODY. La palabra inglesa *prosody*, además de su sentido gramatical (*entonación* y *acentuación*) designa el *arte de la versificación*. (**Shakespeare was a master of prosody.** Shakespeare fue un maestro de la versificación.)

PROSPECTO. *Prospecto* is a *prospectus, brochure,* or *flyer,* if it is one page. (**La oferta de bolsa debe hacerse con un prospecto y no mediante anuncio radiotelefónico.** A stock offering must be made by prospectus and not by a radio announcement.)

PROSPECT, PROSPECTUS. Como sustantivo, *prospect* puede ser un *candidato* o *cliente probable, en perspectiva*. (**The prospect did not buy anything.** El candidato no compró nada.) *Véase también Perspectiva.*

PROYECTO. No significant difference between the Spanish and the English words.

PROJECT. En los Estados Unidos se suele llamar *project* a algo que ya ha pasado la etapa del proyecto: *un barrio de casas nuevas*, por ejemplo. (**He lived in a project just built to improve a poor area.** Vivía en un barrio acabado de construir para mejorar una zona pobre.)

PRUDENTE. *Prudente* and *prudent* are perfect equivalents. (**Es prudente en materia de negocios.** He is prudent in business.)

PRUDE, PRUDENT. *Prude* es *mojigato, gazmoño*. (**He is a prude about what he reads or sees in the movies.** Es mojigato por lo que toca a lo que lee o ve en el cine.)

PSÍQUICO. *Psíquico* means *psychological*. (**Sufre un mal psíquico.** He is affected by a psychological disorder.)

PSYCHIC, PSYCHO. En el uso popular de los Estados Unidos, *psychic* es la *adivina, clarividente*. (**The psychic announced her business by card.** La clarividente anunció su negocio mediante una tarjeta.) *Psycho* es aféresis de *psychopath*, *sicópata*. (**He is an incurable psycho.** Es un sicópata incurable.)

PUBLICANO. Among the Romans, the *publicano* had the concession of collecting public taxes or State mine fees. (**Hacienda es el publicano moderno.** The Treasury is the modern tax collector.)

PUBLICAN. *Publican* es el propietario de un pub (*public house*). O sea, *tabernero, cantinero*. (**The publican knew all his clientele by name.** El tabernero conocía por su nombre a todos los clientes.)

PUEBLO. *Pueblo, localidad, aldea* may be translated as *village, town,* even *hamlet,* that is, just a few houses (*caserío*). (**En el pueblo quedaron muy pocos habitantes.** There were just a few inhabitants left in the village.) *Pueblo* also defines a society characterized by ethnicity or political unity. (**El pueblo sudafricano alcanzó la democracia.** The South African people attained democracy.)

PEOPLE. *People* es *gente.* (**Some people never left their village.** Hay gente que nunca salió de su pueblo.)

PUERTO. *Puerto* and *port* are equivalents, except when *puerto* is used with the meaning of a *pass between mountains, the highest point of a road in a mountainous area.* (**La etapa del Tour de Francia incluía varios puertos de primera categoría.** The stage of the Tour de France included several class A mountain passes.)

PORT.

PUNTO. *Punto* means *point, mark, item, stitch. Al punto* means *at once.*

POINT. Cuando se dice *I would like to make a point*, se trata de expresar *Quiero hacer una observación*, o *aducir un argumento. A point well taken* significa *Su observación es bien fundada* o *Se toma nota de su justo comentario.*

PUPILO. The Spanish word *pupilo* designates a person who has a guardian. It is also a young man housed in a school or a guest house. *Pupila* is a *prostitute*. (**Su hijo era pupilo en el instituto.** Her son was a boarding school student.)

PUPIL. *Pupil* es *alumno*, en general de enseñanza primaria o media. (**Each class had no more than twenty pupils.** No había en cada aula más de veinte alumnos.)

PUZZLE. It is difficult to understand why in Spain *rompecabezas*, the perfect word for this game of assembling differently shaped parts, has been abandoned in favor of an English word that neither adds nor subtracts anything. (**El rompecabezas tenía muchas piezas de muy distinta forma.** The puzzle had many pieces of quite different form.)

PUZZLE. La palabra inglesa, además del *rompecabezas*, designa algo *enigmático, misterioso, enredado, que provoca perplejidad*. (**The operation plan was a puzzle for the laymen.** El plan de operaciones era enigmático para un lego.)

QUIETO. *Quieto* is *still, without movement*. (**Estáte quieto, que quiero tomarte una fotografía.** Don't move, I want to take your picture.)

QUIET. No es que cese el movimiento, sino la palabra. *Quiet* quiere decir *callado, tímido*. (**Be quiet!** Cállate!)

QUINTA. *Quinta* is *a recreation house in the country*. (**En la quinta había caballos y campos de juego.** The country house had playing fields and horses.) It also means *a conscript soldier class*. (**Carlos ingresará con la quinta del año próximo.** Carlos will be conscripted next year.)

QUINT. *Quint* es abreviatura de *quintuplets* (*quintillizos*). (**He is a Smith quint.** Es uno de los quintillizos Smith.)

QUITAR. *Quitar* means *to remove, to delete*. (**Han quitado el cartel de acceso al museo.** The sign indicating the access to the museum has been removed.)

QUIT. *To quit* es *abandonar, dejar*, por ejemplo, de fumar. (**Mark Twain said it was easy to quit smoking. He did it two hundred times.** Mark Twain decía que era fácil dejar de fumar. Él lo había hecho doscientas veces.)

RARO. In Spanish *raro* means *strange, queer, peculiar*. (**Tiene muy raros hábitos.** He has very strange habits.)

RARE. *Rare* es *poco común, inusitado*. (**That was a rare opportunity to see wild animals.** Fue una oportunidad poco común de ver animales salvajes.) También indica *carne poco cocida*. (**I want my steak rare.** Quiero el bistec apenas cocido.)

READ (TO). Se emplea este verbo por *estudiar una materia* en la universidad (uso inglés) y también para *registrar* lo que indica un aparato medidor. (**In college, he read chemistry.** Estudió química en la universidad.)

REAL. Apart from meaning *authentic, true*, in Spanish *real* is the equivalent of *royal*. (**La familia real viajó a provincias.** The royal family traveled to the province.)

REAL. Sinónimo de *auténtico, genuino*. (**I do not like substitutes, I prefer the real thing.** No me gustan los substitutos, prefiero el artículo auténtico.)

REALIZAR. *Realizar*, although slowly assuming the meaning noted in the right-hand column (*to come to understand*), means *to fulfill*, *to make*, *to carry out*, and in economic terms *to sell*, *to make money off of something*. (**Realizó su sueño de viajar al Caribe.** He fulfilled his dream of traveling to the Caribbean. **Logró realizar sus acciones con poca pérdida.** He managed not to lose too much by selling his shares.)

REALIZE. Es común el empleo de este verbo en el sentido de *darse cuenta*, *comprender*. (**Finally, he realized what was good for him and married the girl.** Finalmente, se dio cuenta de lo que le convenía y se casó con esa chica.)

REBATIR. *Rebatir* is *to refute*, *to contest* or *dispute* an assertion, a proposition, or argument. (**Rebatió enérgicamente la pretensión del político.** He energetically refuted the claim of the politician.)

REBATE. *Rebate* es *rebaja*. (**Auto dealers offer rebates to promote new models.** Los concesionarios de automóviles ofrecen rebajas para promover los modelos nuevos.)

RECIDIVA. In medical terms, *recidiva* is rendered by *relapse*. (**El paciente sufrió una recidiva.** The patient had a relapse.)

RECIDIVISM. *Recidivism* significa *reincidencia*. (**There should be an increased punishment in case of recidivism.** Debería aumentarse la pena en caso de reincidencia.)

RECLUSO. In Spanish, *recluso* is a person condemned to *reclusión*, i.e., *preso* (*prisoner*). (**El recluso no recibía visitas.** The convict did not receive visitors.)

RECLUSE. *Recluse* es un *anacoreta*, un *ermitaño*. (**Since the day he lost his wife, he lived as a recluse.** Desde que perdió a su mujer, vivió como un ermitaño.) El adjetivo derivado, significa *apartado*, *solitario*. (**A reclusive place to live.** Un sitio apartado para vivir.)

RECOLECTAR. *Recolectar*, a synonym of *recaudar*, means *to gather, to collect*. (**En la fiesta se recolectó mucho dinero para beneficencia.** At the party, a lot of money was collected for charity.)

RECOLLECT. *To recollect* es *recordar, rememorar*. (**It was the time to recollect past achievements.** Era el momento de rememorar viejas conquistas.)

RECONOCER. Several meanings coincide in the two languages. (**Reconoció su error.** He recognized his mistake. **Los países recién independizados fueron reconocidos de inmediato.** The newly independent countries were immediately recognized.)

RECOGNIZE. En un cuerpo colegiado o en una reunión, *to recognize* es *dar la palabra*. (**At the meeting, the chairman recognizes the delegates.** En la reunión, el presidente da la palabra a los delegados.)

RECORDAR. *Recordar* means *to remember*, not *to record*.

RECORD. *To record* quiere decir *registrar, dejar constancia, tomar nota, grabar*. (**His explanation of vote was recorded.** Se dejó constancia de su explicación de voto.)

RECTOR. Apart from the common meanings of this word, in Spanish *rector*, as an adjective derived from *regir*, means *ruling, governing*. (**La transparencia es un principio rector de la gobernanza.** Transparency is a guiding principle of governance.)

RECTOR. *Rector* suele aplicarse al *director de un seminario* o colegio religioso, y también se designa así a un *párroco*.

RECURRIR. *Recurrir* means to *resort*, *look for help*, or *to appeal* against a decision, judicial or otherwise. (**Recurrió a su mejor amigo en busca de consejo.** He resorted to his best friend for advice. **El demandante recurrió la sentencia.** The plaintiff appealed the sentence.)

RECUR. *Recur* quiere decir *repetirse*, *reiterarse*, *volver*. (**There is a leitmotif that recurs all through the symphony.** Hay un motivo que se repite durante toda la sinfonía.)

RECURRENTE. *Recurrente* is a thing that after being absent reappears. (**Una experiencia recurrente.** An experience that points to the origin of the case.)

RECURRENT, RECURRENCE. *Recurrence* es *reiteración*, *recidiva*. *Recurrent*, *periódico*. (**The recurrence of resolutions year after year lessens their public impact.** La reiteración de resoluciones año a año reduce su eficacia. **A recurrent expenditure.** Un gasto periódico.)

REDUNDANCIA. *Redundancia* is something *superfluous*, *repetitive*. (**Hablar de antiguo arcaísmo es una redundancia.** To speak of an old archaism is a tautology.)

REDUNDANCY. Se habla en el Reino Unido sobre todo de *redundancies* para referirse a *despidos de personal excedente*. (**The reorganization of the firm caused many redundancies.** Por la reorganización de la firma se despidió a mucho personal.)

REEMPLAZAR, SUBSTITUIR. These words mean exactly the same thing in English and Spanish, and their grammatical regimen does not pose problems in Spanish. (**Se reemplaza Gran Bretaña** *por* **el Reino Unido. Hay que sustituir Gran Bretaña** *por* **el Reino Unido.**)

REPLACE, SUBSTITUTE. *Reemplazar* y *substituir* son sinónimos y el régimen gramatical que siguen es diferente en inglés. (**Substitute "the United Kingdom of Great Britain and Northern Ireland"** *for* **"Britain." Replace "Britain"** *by* **"the United Kingdom of Great Britain and Northern Ireland."**)

REFERIR. *Referir* may be *to relate to* or *to narrate, to tell.* (**Como estuvo ausente, le refirió lo hablado en la reunión.** Since he was absent, he told him what was discussed at the meeting.)

REFER. Un médico *refers* un paciente a un especialista, un funcionario, un asunto a una autoridad superior para decisión. Se traduce al español por *remitir* o *transferir.* (**The general practitioner referred him to a urologist.** El médico generalista [*clínico en algunos países*] lo remitio a un urólogo.)

REFINAR. *Refinar* means *to refine, polish, perfect.*

REFINE. *Refine* es también *depurar, purificar, perfeccionar.* (**A refined version of the software was more efficient.** Una versión perfeccionada del programa resultó más eficaz.)

REFLEXIÓN, REFLEJO. These two Spanish words are expressed in English by *reflection.* (**Una reflexión atinada.** A wise reflection. **El reflejo del sol en el agua daba extrañas figuras.** The sun reflected in the water made strange images.)

REFLECTION. (**His reflection in the mirror showed an old man.** El espejo reflejaba un anciano.)

REFRÁN, REFRENAR. *Refrán* is a *proverb.* (**Ese refrán no tiene equivalente en inglés.** That proverb has no equivalent in English.)

REFRAIN. El sustantivo *refrain* quiere decir *estribillo.* (**The song had a catchy refrain.** La canción tenía un estribillo pegadizo.) El verbo *to refrain* significa *contenerse, abstenerse.* (**I refrained from answering his abuse.** Me contuve para no contestar su insulto.)

REGALAR. *Regalar* is *to make a gift* or a present. It is usual just to say *to give*, with "as a present" being understood. (**Le regalaron cosas útiles.** He was given useful things.)

REGALE. *To regale* es *agasajar, festejar.* (**For his birthday, she regaled him with a feast for him and his friends.** Para su cumpleaños, ella lo agasajó con un banquete para él y sus amigos.)

REGISTRAR. *Registrar* may denote *to search.* (**Registraron a todos los pasajeros del vuelo a Tel Aviv.** All passengers of the Tel Aviv flight were searched.)

REGISTER. *To register* tiene habitualmente el significado de *anotar, matricular, hacer constar,* con todas las posibilidades de lenguaje figurado. (**Her face did not register any emotion.** Su rostro no delató emoción ninguna.)

REGULACIÓN. *Regulación* may entail *control.* (**La regulación de alquileres tiende a ayudar a los inquilinos pobres.** Rent control tends to help poor tenants.)

REGULATION. Además de *regulación*, **regulation** quiere decir *reglamento.* (**They act according to regulations.** Actúan según los reglamentos.)

REGULAR. In Spanish this word could mean *fair, so-so.* (**La nueva película era regular.** The new film was so-so.)

REGULAR. *Regular* quiere decir *normal, constante, ordinario, periódico.* (**The regular budget.** El presupuesto ordinario. **A regular feature of this author.** Una característica constante de este autor. **He travels regularly to Europe.** Viaja periódicamente a Europa.)

REHUSAR. *Refuse* and **rehusar** are completely equivalent words.

REFUSE. *Refuse*, como sustantivo, quiere decir *desperdicios, basura.* (***The refuse collection is quite regular.*** La recolección de desperdicios se hace con regularidad.)

RELACIÓN. There are two interesting meanings of *relación* to retain: *ratio* and *listing*. (**Tiene una buena relación entre el "buen" y el "mal" colesterol.** The ratio between "good" and "bad" cholesterol is fine. **Una relación de los hechos.** A listing of events.)

RELATION. No hay diferencias significativas entre las acepciones de las dos palabras.

RELATIVO. *Relativo* most often means *referring to*. (**Un estudio relativo al parentesco.** An essay referring to family relations.)

RELATIVE. *Parientes* son en inglés *relatives*. (**The extended family in Africa may include many relatives.** La familia ampliada de África tal vez incluya a muchos parientes.)

RELEVANTE. In Spanish, *relevante* means *important, outstanding*. (**El deportista etíope tuvo una actuación relevante en atletismo.** The Ethiopian sportsman gave an outstanding performance in athletics.)

RELEVANT. *Relevant* se traduce como *pertinente* y no relevante. (**That article of the rules is relevant to this situation.** Ese artículo del reglamento es pertinente para la situación actual.)

RELEVAR. *Relevar* may mean *to replace someone*, to take his turn in doing some duty. (**Lo relevaba en la vigilancia a medianoche.** He replaced him at midnight to continue the watch.) A related term is *carrera de relevos* or *de postas (relay race)* in some Latin American countries.

RELIEVE, RELIEF. *Relief* es *socorro, auxilio*, en tanto que *relieve* es *relevar*, eximir de una carga. (**After the tsunami, a worldwide relief operation was mounted.** Tras el tsunami, se organizó una operación mundial de socorro. **The accused was relieved of his duties pending the investigation.** Se relevó al acusado de sus obligaciones durante la investigación.)

REMOVER. *Remover* is *to stir.* (**Hay que remover la mezcla cinco minutos.** You have to stir the mix for five minutes.)

REMOVE. *To remove* nunca es *remover,* sino *eliminar, quitar, suprimir.* (**The squatters were forcibly removed from the building.** Los intrusos fueron desalojados por la fuerza del edificio.)

RENTA. *Renta* has been used of late for *arrendamiento* (*rent*) or *alquiler* (*rent*). Other meanings are *income, revenue, return, yield, annuity,* depending on the different cases to which they are applied. (**La renta nacional es un factor determinante de la economía.** National income is a decisive factor in the economy. **No trabaja, vive de rentas.** He does not work, but lives on the income of his investments.)

RENT. *Rent* se usa sobre todo en el sentido de *alquiler,* aunque, con la mano de obra y el capital, tiene el sentido de la tierra como factor de la producción. (**Rent, labor, and capital determine the economy of a country.** La tierra, la mano de obra y el capital deciden la situación económica de un país.)

REPARACIÓN. In Spanish, *reparación* is *repair.* (**Las reparaciones de un Mercedes Benz son costosas.** Repairs of a Mercedes are costly.)

REPARATION. *Reparation* tiene, además del corriente, el sentido de *compensación, resarcimiento.* (**Germany paid reparations to the Jews after World War II.** Alemania pagó indemnizaciones a los judíos después de la segunda guerra mundial.)

REPLICAR. *Replicar* is *to reply, dispute,* or *contest.* (**Le replicó agriamente.** He replied bitterly.)

REPLICATE. *To replicate* significa *repetir una obra o experiencia.* (**The social housing scheme was replicated successfully in other countries.** El plan de vivienda social se repitió con éxito en otros países.)

REPROCHE. The Spanish word means *rebuke* or *disapproval*. (**Su discurso le valió el reproche de sus compañeros.** His words brought him the disapproval of his colleagues.)

REPROACH. *Reproach* quiere decir *censura, oprobio, descrédito.* ***To be above reproach*** quiere decir *sin tacha.* (**The writer had a personal history above reproach.** El escritor tenía una historia personal sin tacha. **A unanimous reproach followed the publication of his second book.** La censura unánime de los críticos acompañó la publicación de su segundo libro.)

REQUERIR. *Requerir* means *to need*, but also *to summon, to court.* (**El juez requirió la presencia del acusado.** The judge summoned the defendant. **Requirió de amores a su vecina.** He courted his neighbor.)

REQUIRE. Una acepción de esta palabra inglesa es *obligar, compeler.* (**The student of English was required to read five works by classical authors.** El estudiante de inglés estaba obligado a leer cinco obras de autores clásicos.)

RESERVA. *Reserva*, in addition to *reserve* and the term in accounting, may mean *reticence* or *misgiving.* (**Mostró reserva ante su sugerencia.** He reacted hesitatingly to his suggestion.) At present, *reservación* is used where *reserva* was employed in the sense of *to make a reservation.*

RESERVE, RESERVOIR. *Reservoir* es una *reserva*, un *depósito*, incluso en sentido figurado (*a reservoir of good faith*, una disposición de buena fe), *embalse* o *pantano.* (**Because of the drought, most reservoirs are at a fraction of their capacity.** Debido a la sequía, la mayoría de los embalses están con la capacidad reducida.)

RESOLUCIÓN, RESOLVER. *Resolver* means *to settle, to solve, to arrive at a resolution* of something. (**El conflicto de intereses se resolvió satisfactoriamente en la empresa.** The conflict of interest was satisfactorily resolved at the company.)

RESOLUTION, RESOLVE. *Resolution* y *resolve* son sinónimos en el sentido de *tesón, determinación, decisión.* (**The President showed his resolve to combat terrorism.** El Presidente mostró su determinación de combatir el terrorismo.) Una *resolution* es una decisión con distinta fuerza jurídica según su origen. (**At the UN, most resolutions are not compulsory.** En la ONU, la mayoría de las resoluciones no tiene fuerza ejecutoria.) *New Year's resolutions* son las promesas que para el próximo año se formula la gente.

RESPONSABLE. *Responsable* may be used in the sense of *reliable.* (**En materia de horarios, es muy responsable.** He is very reliable in keeping timetables.)

RESPONSIBLE. A menudo se dice *responsible* por quien está a cargo de un puesto o determinada tarea, sin implicar responsabilidad jurídica o moral. (**Diana is responsible for the preparation of the guest list.** Diana tiene a su cargo la preparación de la lista de invitados.) En términos jurídicos, *liable* indica que alguien o alguna empresa es responsable. *LLC, limited liability corporation,* es *sociedad de responsabilidad limitada.*

RESTAR, RESTO. In Spanish, *restar* is *to subtract*, and *resto*, always in mathematics, is *remainder*. The plural *restos* (*mortales*) means *remains*. (**Restar es una de las cuatro operaciones aritméticas básicas.** Subtracting is one of the four basic arithmetic operations. **Una division exacta no deja resto.** An exact division leaves no remainder. **Los restos del difunto fueron enterrados ayer.** The remains of the deceased were buried yesterday.)

REST. Entre las muchísimas acepciones de *rest* que pueden interesar por su relación con voces inglesas están las de *concluir la presentación de un alegato* (**The counsel rested his case.** El letrado terminó su presentación.), *base*, *apoyo* (*a rest for his feet*, escabel, *apoyo para los pies*) y una palabra en español que pocos recuerdan: *los demás*, para decir *the rest*.

RESTAURAR. For *restaurar un cuadro*, the verb used is *to restore*. (**La Capilla Sixtina fue reabierta completada la restauración de la bóveda.** The Sistine Chapel was reopened once the restoration of the ceiling was completed.)

RESTORE. *Restore* puede querer decir *restablecer*. (**The government restored the tax on food.** El gobierno restableció el impuesto sobre los alimentos.) *Restaurar* a alguien en su cargo se expresa con el verbo *to reinstate*.

RESUMEN, RESUMIR. *Resumir* is *to sum up* or *condense*. (**Resumió en pocas páginas sus ideas.** He condensed his ideas in a few pages. **Hizo un resumen del libro.** He summarized the book.)

RESUME, RESUMÉ. *To resume* quiere decir *reanudar*. (**After one hour's recess, the President resumed the session.** Tras un receso de una hora, el Presidente reanudó la session.) *Resumé* es la lista de aptitudes, educación y experiencia de trabajo, que en español se suele expresar con la expresión *currículum vitae* o *cv*.

RETIRAR, RETIRO. *Retiro* is a synonym of *jubilación* meaning *retirement*. *Retirar* is *to withdraw*. (**La multinacional retiró su oferta de compra de la empresa china.** The multinational corporation withdrew its offer to buy the Chinese company.)

RETIRE, RETREAT. *To retire* es *jubilarse*. (**Civil servants retire at age 65.** Los empleados públicos se jubilant a los 65 años.) La palabra *retreat* está hoy en boga porque describe tambien una reunión en un lugar retirado a fin de meditar o discutir asuntos importantes sin la presión del trabajo diario. (**They organized a retreat in the mountains to deal with sales.** Organizaron un retiro en la montaña para hablar de ventas.)

RETRIBUCIÓN. In Spanish, this word has only a positive connotation, generally of a *monetary compensation*. (**La retribución por su trabajo es suficiente.** The remuneration for his work is adequate.)

RETRIBUTION. *Retribution* denota las consecuencias de acciones, y puede entonces significar *recompensa* o *castigo*. (**He must have expected such retribution.** Esperaba con seguridad esa retribución.)

REUNIÓN. In Spanish, a *reunión* is any meeting.

REUNION. En inglés, *reunion* se usa casi exclusivamente para una *reunión evocativa*, una celebración de aniversario o un reencuentro después de muchos años, por ejemplo, en *family reunion*, que puede incluir a miembros de varias generaciones, separados geográficamente. Como el término es español, en la traducción hace falta hacer la calificación.

Rico. *Rico* is *tasty, delighful* in colloquial Spanish. (**El más rico de los postres.** The tastiest of desserts.)

Rich. Dicho de un alimento, *rich* quiere decir *graso o con muchas calorías*. (**That course is too rich for my diet.** Ese plato es excesivo para mi régimen.)

Rodeo. *Hablar con rodeos* means *to turn in circles to avoid saying something directly*, or to define something in a convoluted way. (**Ser claro y no dar rodeos.** To speak clearly without beating around the bush.)

Rodeo. Los vaqueros (*cowboys*) americanos tomaron del español la palabra *rodeo* para designar una feria de ganado y competencias de destreza con caballos, toros, en que participan. (**The rodeo is typical of the western United States.** El rodeo es típico del oeste estadounidense.)

Rudo. *Rudo*, in Spanish, is *coarse, dull, primitive.* (**Un hombre rudo, pero bondadoso.** He is a bit unpolished, but a good soul.)

Rude. Tal vez el uso más común de *rude* sea con el sentido de *grosero o descortés*. (**He addressed the lady very rudely.** Se dirigió a la dama de manera muy grosera.)

Ruptura. No special remarks about the usage of these perfectly equivalent terms.

Rupture. *Rupture* puede querer decir *hernia*. (**He was very uncomfortable because of a rupture.** Se sentía muy incómodo a raíz de la hernia.)

Saludar, Saludo. *Saludo*, unless it is of the military type (*salute*), means *greeting(s)*. (**Saludos desde mi retiro de vacaciones.** Greetings from my holiday retreat.)

Salute. *To salute* es *saludar, celebrar, dar la bienvenida, hacer la venia*. (**The cooperative board saluted the decision to subsidize a swimming pool.** La cooperativa del edificio celebró la decisión de subvencionar la piscina.)

SALVAR. *Salvar* is equivalent to *to save* or *to rescue*. (**El náufrago fue salvado por otro buque.** Shipwrecked, he was rescued by another ship.)

SALVAGE. *To salvage* es *recuperar, rescatar* mercancías de un desastre. (**Nothing could be salvaged from the sunken ship.** No pudo recuperarse nada del buque hundido.)

SANEAMIENTO, SANIDAD. *Saneamiento* means *sanitation*, and *sanidad, hygiene* or *health services.* (**Entre los organismos internacionales, Habitat estudia el saneamiento urbano, y la Organización Mundial de la Salud la sanidad.** Among the international organizations, Habitat deals with urban sanitation and the World Health Organization with hygiene.)

SANITATION. *Sanitation* quiere decir *saneamiento, salubridad,* el cuidado de la higiene en los núcleos de habitación. (**Many developing countries lack adequate sanitation services.** Muchos países en desarrollo carecen de servicios adecuados de saneamiento.)

SANGUÍNEO, SANGUINARIO. *Grupo sanguíneo* is *blood type. Sanguinario* is *sanguinary, blood-thirsty.*

SANGUINE. *Sanguine,* además de aludir al color sangre de la piel, por ejemplo, es un *optimista.* Tiene la actitud de quien confía en que ocurrirá lo que espera. (**I am not too sanguine about launching this project.** No tengo muchas esperanzas en cuanto a este nuevo proyecto.)

SANIDAD. *See Saneamiento.*

SANITY. *Sanity* deriva de *sane, cuerdo.* (**Sometimes you feel that sanity is a rare commodity.** A veces piensas que la cordura es un artículo poco común.)

SATISFACER. Practically no major difference between the two terms.

SATISFY. En inglés, la expresión *to be satisfied with* significa *convencerse* de algo. (**He was satisfied that the evidence was overwhelming.** Estaba convencido de que las pruebas eran abrumadoras.)

SECULAR. *Secular* has two meanings common to both languages. We wish to list them here because they may cause confusion: one is *temporal, earthly*, as opposed to *holy*, and the other *age-old*.

SECULAR. Las acepciones coinciden en ambas lenguas, pero para evitar confusiones, conviene repetirlo: *secular*, o *seglar,* es *temporal*, por oposición a *sagrado*, y la otra, *centenario*.

SECUNDAR, ADSCRIBIR. *Secundar* means *to support*. (**Lo secundó en su plan.** He supported him on his plan.)

SECOND. *To second* es *secundar* o *apoyar*, pero también *adscribir*, o sea *asignar personal* propio a un servicio o empleo. (**The motion by France was seconded by Germany.** La moción de Francia fue apoyada por Alemania. **The lawyer was seconded from the Legal Office to the Personnel Department.** El abogado fue adscripto de la Oficina Jurídica al Departamento de Personal.)

SEMÁFORO. A *semáforo* in the city is called a *traffic light* in the United States, reserving *semaphore* for the lights used to direct railroad traffic. (**Los semáforos están dispuestos internacionalmente en cierto orden, para prevenir los accidentes con daltónicos.** Internationally, traffic lights are arranged in a certain order, to prevent accidents involving color blind people.)

SEMAPHORE. *Semaphore*, como decimos al lado, se utiliza en los recorridos ferroviarios. (**Semaphores change automatically thanks to devices placed on the tracks.** Los semáforos cambian automáticamente debido a dispositivos colocados en las vías.)

SENSIBLE. *Sensible* is translated into English as *sensitive*. (**Es muy sensible a los sufrimientos de los animales.** He is very sensitive to animal suffering.)

SENSIBLE, SENSITIVE. En inglés, *sensible* quiere decir *razonable*; *sensitive* es el equivalente del español *sensible*. (**That was the sensible thing to do.** Era lo más razonable por hacer.)

SENTENCIA. *Sentencia* is the decision of a court. (**La sentencia podría ser absolutoria.** The sentence might be an acquittal.)

SENTENCE. *Sentence* en inglés tiene por lo general un sentido negativo, de *condena*, en tanto que en español es neutral: *fallo, juicio, decisión*. (**The sentence will be carried out immediately.** La sentencia se ejecutará de inmediato.) Además, gramaticalmente *sentence* es *oración*.

SEPARADO, SEPARATA. *Separado* means *apart*, *estranged*. (**Los cónyuges están separados.** The spouses are estranged.) *Separata* is the single reprint of a press article, a chapter of a book, etc. (**Hizo una separata de su última comunicación científica.** He published copies of his latest scientific essay.)

SEPARATE. *Separate* indica algo no solamente aparte, sino también *privado, propio de uno.* (**He finally obtained a separate office.** Por fin, obtuvo una oficina propia.)

SERIO. *Serio* may be rendered as *thoughtful, dependable, solemn, grave, responsible.* (**Es un estudiante serio.** He is a responsible student.)

SERIOUS. *Serious* se traduce por *sincero, formal* y *grave* en el caso de enfermedad. (**His condition was quite serious.** Su estado era bastante grave. **He met a serious clerk.** Conoció a un oficinista formal. **He has a serious countenance.** Tiene un semblante grave.)

SESIÓN. *Sesión* and *reunión* are equivalent terms. Their use is a matter of convention.

SESSION. Igual que en el caso de *commission* y *committee*, en el caso de *session* y *meeting* la distinción es convencional. En las Naciones Unidas, por ejemplo, se usa *meeting* para una reunión individual y *session* para una serie de reuniones en un período determinado.

SIMPATÍA. It is difficult sometimes to translate the notion of *simpatía*. It can be *niceness, congeniality* or some other term according to the context. (**La novia fue elogiada por su simpatía.** The bride won praise for her congeniality.)

SYMPATHY. Expresar *sympathy* a alguien es *darle el pésame, condolencias* por un fallecimiento. (**The President expressed his sympathy to the families of the victims of the terrorist attack.** El Presidente expresó sus condolencias a las familias de las víctimas del atentado terrorista.)

SIMPÁTICO. *Simpático* is *kind*, *nice*, difficult to render as we already noted. (**Su novio es un tipo simpático.** Her fiancé is a nice guy.)

SYMPATHETIC. *Sympathetic* quiere decir *compasivo*. (**He is always sympathetic with handicapped people.** Es siempre compasivo con los minusválidos.) *Sympathetic nervous system* es *el sistema del gran simpático*.

SINDICATO. In Spanish, *sindicato* is *trade union*, or, more simply, *union*. (**Unions are very powerful in France.** Los sindicatos son muy poderosos en Francia.)

SYNDICATE. En periodismo, se usa la palabra *syndicate* para significar una organización o persona que difunde el mismo material a diversos medios de comunicación. (**His syndicated column appeared in 60 papers nationwide.** Su columna había sido contratada para aparecer en 60 periódicos de todo el país.)

SINIESTRA, SINIESTRO. Derived from the Latin *sinister*, this means *on the left side* or *unlucky*. *Siniestra* means *left* (*a diestra y siniestra*, everywhere). *Siniestro* is also the *damage* covered in an insurance contract. (**El siniestro abarcó la pérdida total del bien asegurado.** The damage was the total loss of the insured asset.)

SINISTER. *Sinister* es sinónimo de *ominous*, *evil*. (**He was tormented by a sinister foreboding.** Le atormentaba una predicción siniestra.)

SIRVIENTE, SERVIDOR. *Un sirviente* is whoever serves his master. (**El sirviente tenía maneras refinadas.** The servant had refined manners.) *Un servidor* means the person who is speaking. (**José Pérez, un servidor.** Yours truly, José Pérez.)

SERVANT. *Civil servant* es un funcionario de la administración de un país o de una organización internacional. (**The civil servants of the UN make up the Secretariat.** Los funcionarios de las Naciones Unidas integran la Secretaría.)

SOLICITANTE. A *solicitante* is an *applicant*. (**El solicitante tenía los documentos en regla.** The applicant had all documents in order.)

SOLICITATION, SOLICITOR. El *solicitor* es un *abogado* o *procurador*, no un solicitante. (**The defendant was accompanied by his solicitor.** El demandado estaba acompañado por su abogado.) *To solicit* puede emplearse por instar a conceder algo (*solicit donations*, *requerir donaciones*) o, como *solicitation*, para el acoso de una prostituta.

SOLICITUD. Apart from the meanings common to both words, *solicitud* is also *application form*. (**La solicitud incluye muchos datos personales.** The application form includes a lot of personal data.)

SOMBRERO. Los tejanos sobre todo han incorporado a su léxico esta palabra española, pero con el sentido específico de sombrero de su propio estilo.

SOPORTAR. *Soportar* means *to endure, to put up with, to suffer*. (**Europa soportó una gran ola de calor.** Europe suffered an intense heat wave.)

SUPPORT, SUPPORTER. *To support* es *apoyar*. En términos deportivos y en el uso inglés, un *supporter* es un *hincha, forofo, tifoso, fan* o *partidario,* por lo general de un equipo de fútbol. (**English supporters travel long distances with their touring teams.** Los hinchas ingleses viajan lejos con sus equipos en gira.)

SOSPECHA, SOSPECHOSO, SUSPICACIA, SUSPICAZ. *Sospecha* and *suspicacia* may both be translated as *suspicion*, but they have shades of meaning, as illustrated in the column to the right. *Sospechoso* and *suspicaz* are adjectives that correspond to *sospecha* and *suspicacia*.

SUSPICION, SUSPICIOUS. El traductor tal vez dude si traducir *suspicion* por *sospecha* o *suspicacia*. (**He was arrested on suspicion of fraud.** Lo arrestaron sospechoso de fraude. **The buyer reacted with suspicion to the latest offer.** El comprador mostró suspicacia ante la última oferta.) En sentido figurado y en el uso inglés, *suspicion* puede ser *una pizca* de un ingrediente. (**The recipe called for a suspicion of clove.** La receta pedía una pizca de clavo de olor.)

SPANGLISH. A broad term used to refer to the blend of Spanish and English spoken by Spanish and Latin American immigrants to the United States who, just like those who went to Germany, Switzerland, or France, created a hybrid jargon to cope with a different social and working environment. Spanglish uses a variety of linguistic phenomena, including code switching, word borrowings from English into Spanish, using false cognates with their English sense, and calquing idiomatic English expressions. *Subir al rufo para fijar la boila* replaces *Subir al techo para arreglar la caldera*; instead of call me back, *llámame para atrás*, and *una caja corta*, *por una caja de menos*.

SPANGLISH. Se denomina Spanglish al habla popular especialmente de la mano de obra española y latinoamericana, que mezcla palabras y expresiones inglesas con otras españolas. Casos similares de mezcla con el alemán y el francés existen en Alemania, Francia y Suiza. Rechazado por los puristas como un español corrupto, hay que reconocer que se utiliza en hospitales, servicios sociales, la iglesia, etc. Por ahora no se le acuerda la jerarquía de sus nobles antecesores, el judeoespañol nacido del castellano, y las lenguas romances, originadas en el latín de las legiones romanas.

SUBSTANCIA. The basic meanings in both languages are the same.

SUBSTANCE. *Substance* es *el fondo*, por oposición a la forma (*form* o *shape*). (**The substance of the matter is poverty.** El fondo de la cuestión es la pobreza.) *A person of substance* es una persona adinerada. Cuando algo *lacks substance,* es que no se justifica o no corresponde a la realidad. *Substance abuse* es una manera eufemística de referirse al abuso de drogas o alcohol. (**The autopsy revealed substance abuse.** La nautopsia reveló abuso de drogas.)

SUCEDER. *Suceder* is *to happen* or *to be a successor*. (**Al Presidente Clinton sucedió el Presidente Bush.** President Clinton was succeeded by President Bush. **Sucedió mientras dormía.** It happened while he was asleep.)

SUCCEED. Aparte de *ser sucesor*, *to succeed* quiere decir *tener éxito*. (**He succeeded where others failed.** Tuvo éxito en lo que otros fracasaron.)

SUCESO. *Suceso* may be the news "from the police blotter" (*a criminal occurrence or an accident*) or simply an *event*. (**Prefería empezar por leer la crónica de sucesos.** He preferred to start by reading the police chronicle. **Ha sido un suceso desafortunado.** It was an unfortunate occurrence.)

SUCCESS. *Success* es *éxito* y no *suceso*. (**The book on Barcelona was a big success.** El libro sobre Barcelona tuvo mucho éxito.)

SUERTE. *Suerte* means *luck, fate, lot.* (**La suerte quiso que ganara.** Luck had it that he would win.) It may be a synonym of *sort*: *una suerte de aparato* (a kind of device). It also refers to the stages of a bullfight. (**El torero realizó varias suertes.** The toreador performed several stages.)

SORT. *Sort* es *clase, carácter, variedad.* (**I prefer this sort of work.** Prefiero este tipo de trabajo.) Como verbo, *to sort* es *separar, clasificar en grupos.* (**The employee sorts cards according to profession.** El empleado separa las tarjetas según las profesiones.)

SUFICIENTE. *Suficiente* is a synonym of *pedantic.* (**Su actitud suficiente lo malquistó con la gente.** His pedantic attitude alienated him from the people.)

SUFFICIENT. Ya vimos que *sufficient*, que significa *bastante*, puede ser sinónimo de *adequate.* (**Sufficient money was collected at the fair.** Se recaudó bastante dinero en la feria.)

SUFRAGIO. *Sufragio* means *vote*, or in its religious meaning *vow.* (**Pidió un sufragio por las almas de los difuntos del pueblo.** He made an offering for the souls of the deceased of the village.) *Sufragio universal* is that given to all citizens, men and women.

SUFFRAGE. *Suffrage* significa tanto el *voto* como el *derecho de voto.* (cf. *Franchise*)

SUGERENCIA, SUGESTIÓN. One has to be very careful in translating *suggestion*, because it may mean one of two different things: *sugerencia*, as *the action of suggesting,* or *sugestión*, a psychological term that denotes *the influence that alters the normal judgment of someone.* (**Su sugerencia fue tenida en cuenta.** His suggestion was well taken. **Ejercía una sugestión malsana sobre mi hermano.** He had an unhealthy influence over my brother.)

SUGGESTION. Tanto *sugerencia* como *sugestión* se traducen en ingles por *suggestion*.

Sugerir. *Sugerir* and *insinuar* share the same meaning, *to suggest*. (**Le sugirió reunirse en el centro comercial.** He suggested a meeting at the mall.)

Suggest. *To suggest* quiere decir *traer a la memoria, insinuar, inspirar, proponer.* (**John suggested the idea to him.** John le insinuó la idea.)

Sujeto. *Sujeto* is an *individual*, but the word may be used with a pejorative connotation. (**Un sujeto indeseable.** An undesirable individual.)

Subject. *Subject* es *súbdito*, dependiente de un superior. Suele aplicarse a ciudadano, aunque un país como el Reino Unido tiene *subjects* de Su Majestad que no son necesariamente ciudadanos del Reino Unido. (**He is a subject of Her British Majesty, citizen of Canada.** Es un súbdito de Su Majestad. Británica, ciudadano del Canadá.)

Sumario. In Spanish, apart from the common meanings, *sumario* indicates the series of judicial or police actions in preparation of a trial. (**El sumario preparado por la policía llenaba cincuenta páginas.** The file prepared by the police filled fifty pages.)

Summary. *Summary* y *sumario* significan lo mismo: *resumen, índice. Véase Resumir.*

Tarifa. *Tarifa* is *rate, a schedule of prices.* (**El ayuntamiento exige que se exhiba la tarifa de reparaciones.** The city requires the schedule of repair prices to be displayed at the store.)

Tariff. *Tariff* significa específicamente *aranceles, derechos aduaneros.* (**The World Trade Organization succeeded the General Agreement on Trade and Tariffs.** La Organización Internacional del Comercio sucedió al Acuerdo General sobre Aranceles y Comercio.)

TENTATIVA. *Tentativa* means *attempt.* (**Fue una tentativa de robo.** It was attempted burglary.)

TENTATIVE. *Tentative* es un adjetivo que quiere decir *provisional, probable.* (**A tentative date was set for the next meeting.** Se estableció una fecha provisional para la próxima reunión.) También significa *vacilante, incierto.* (**Her reaction was a tentative smile.** Reaccionó con una sonrisa vacilante.)

TERGIVERSAR. In Spanish this word is used mainly in the sense of *distort, misrepresent.* (**Sus palabras tergiversaban el sentido del homenaje.** His discourse twisted the meaning of the tribute.)

TERGIVERSATE. *To tergiversate* quiere decir también *apostatar, renegar.* (**After his misfortune, he tergiversated from his faith.** Después de su desgracia, renegó de su fe.)

TERMINAR. No special comment about the word **terminar**.

TERMINATE. En inglés, *to terminate* es un verbo transitivo que significa *dar por terminado, rescindir, revocar.* (**His contract was terminated before the agreed-upon date.** Su contrato fue rescindido antes de la fecha convenida.)

TERSO. *Terso* means *silky, smooth,* and speaking of writing style, *fluid.* (**Tiene una piel tersa.** She has soft skin.)

TERSE. *Terse* se traduce al español por *sucinto, conciso.* (**In a terse statement, the mayor acknowledged the criticism.** En una breve declaración, el alcalde reconoció las críticas. **The author depicts the atmosphere in a terse style.** El autor describe el ambiente con toda fluidez.)

Tiempo real. Equivalent to the English phrase (*in*) *real time.* (**Las cotizaciones se dan en tiempo real.** Quotations are given immediately, as they happen.)

Real time. Encuentro que *real time*, que ha pasado al uso mediático en su traducción literal, es algo que ocurre, o se trasmite o difunde, *instantáneamente, en el momento* y no demorado, más tarde (*delayed*).

Tópico. A *tópico* may be a medicine applied locally, like an *ointment*, but it also means *commonplace* and *subject*. (**Su clase no valía mucho: estaba llena de tópicos.** His class was not worth much, it was mostly commonplace. **El tópico del día es Rembrandt.** The topic today is Rembrandt.)

Topical. *Topical* significa *actual, corriente.* (**Terrorism is a very topical subject.** El terrorismo es un asunto de gran actualidad.)

Traducir, Trasladar. *Trasladar*, most likely the word that originated the others mentioned here, means *to move, to change* or *transfer.* (**Se trasladó a un lugar más cercano a su domicilio.** He moved to a place closer to home.)

Traduce, Translate. *Traduce* no es *traducir* (*to translate*) sino *calumniar, difamar.* (**Traduced by his neighbor, he sued him for libel.** Difamado por su vecino, lo demandó por injurias. **To be able to translate Shakespeare, you have to be a poet yourself.** Para poder traducir a Shakespeare, tienes que ser poeta.)

Trampa. *Trampa* is translated as *trap, snare*, or *pitfall.* (**Los estudiantes de inglés suelen caer en las trampas del idioma.** Students of English often fall into the traps of the language.) *Hacer trampa* is *to cheat.* (**Con cartas o dados, siempre hacía trampa.** Dice or cards, he always cheated.)

Tramp. *Tramp* es *vagabundo* o *ramera.* (**The tramp looked for food in the garbage cans.** El vagabundo buscaba alimento en los cilindros de la basura.)

TRASCENDENTAL. In Spanish, *trascendental* is something that has an extraordinary importance, which will have far-reaching results. (**Los esposos Curie hicieron un descubrimiento trascendental.** Mr. and Mrs. Curie made an extraordinary discovery.)

TRANSCENDENTAL. *Transcendental* se utiliza a veces para significar *sobrenatural*. (**This mystic group studies the transcendental.** Este grupo místico estudia lo sobrenatural.) También se refiere a la doctrina flosófica conocida como *transcendentalism* (o *trascendentalismo*) que afirma la primacía de lo espiritual sobre lo físico. (**His transcendental ideas governed his ethics.** Su ideario trascendental regía su moral.)

TRASPASAR. *Traspasar* may mean *to cross*, *to pierce*, or in military language, *to overrun an outpost*. (**El duelista lo traspasó con su espada.** The duelist pierced him with his sword. **Traspasó los límites del buen gusto.** He crossed the boundaries of taste.)

TRESPASS. *Trespass* quiere decir *penetrar sin derecho*, como intruso, trasgredir un límite. (**Private property: no trespassing.** Propiedad privada: prohibido el paso.)

TREN. *Tren de aterrizaje* is not a train, but the *landing gear* of a plane.

TRAIN. *Train of thought* es *la secuencia de ideas* o razonamiento que conduce a una conclusión.

TRUCULENTO. These are perfect synonyms.

TRUCULENT. En inglés, *truculent*, además de *truculento*, significa *agresivo, belicoso, insolente*. (**The customer had a truculent disposition.** El cliente tenía una actitud belicosa.)

TUTOR. This is the word generally used in Spanish for a *legal guardian*. (**El juez designa a tutores de menores y de incapaces.** The judge appoints guardians for minors and the legally incompetent.) *Tutor* is also a *stake* (plant support or reinforcement). (**El pino joven necesitaba un tutor.** The young pine tree required a stake.)

TUTOR. *Tutor* es *el maestro* que da clases particulares y se emplea también para profesores asistentes. El verbo *to tutor* se emplea también en estos casos. (**He was a tutor of English at Oxford.** Era tutor de inglés en Oxford.)

ÚLTIMO. *Último* means nothing more than *last*. *Por último* means *finally*.

ULTIMATE. *Ultimate* tiene la connotación de cosa definitiva, de algo óptimo, no sólo de último lugar. (**His company manufactures the ultimate product for the prevention of baldness.** Su compañía fabrica el producto más moderno para prevenir la calvicie.)

ULTRAJE. *Ultraje* is a synonym of *injuria* (*offense*), *afrenta* (*insult*), *ofensa* (*offense*). (**Esa película es un ultraje al pudor.** That film is an insult to modesty.)

OUTRAGE. *Outrage* puede querer decir *atrocidad* o *indignación*, *cólera* como consecuencia. (**The recent terrorist acts were an outrage.** Los recientes actos terroristas fueron una atrocidad. **Tomb desecration is an outrage to humanity.** La profanación de tumbas es un crimen de lesa humanidad.)

ULTRAMARINO. There are meanings common to both languages, *overseas, beyond the seas.* A doubly historical meaning in the case of Spanish: ***tienda de ultramarinos*** in other times used to sell products coming from across the ocean (***ultramar***), but that is now rendered obsolete by the modern supermarket.

ULTRAMARINE.

ÚNICO. *Único* is sometimes rendered as *sole.* (**La única razón de su viaje fue ver a un artista famoso.** The sole reason for her trip was to see a famous artist.)

UNIQUE. *Unique* se traduce por *singular*, ya que designa a algo que sale de lo común. (**That jewel had a unique kind of tanzanite.** Esa joya tenía una tanzanita muy peculiar.)

UNIÓN. Nothing special to note about this pair of analogous words.

UNION. *Trade union*, o sencillamente ***union***, es específicamente un *sindicato*. (**From their United Kingdom headquarters, the International Confederation of Free Trade Unions leads very important labor campaigns.** Desde su sede en el Reino Unido, la Confederación Internacional de Organizaciones Sindicales Libres lleva a cabo campañas laborales muy importantes.)

URBANIZACIÓN. *Urbanización* is the phenomenon of the growth and relative proportion of cities in the demography of a country. (**La urbanización de muchos países les plantea serios problemas de infraestructura.** In many countries, urbanization poses many infrastructure problems.) An *urbanización* is also a *housing complex*, frequently of secondary residences, in a summer or leisure place. (**Urbanizaciones de lujo abundan en la costa española.** Luxury developments dot the Spanish coast.)

URBANIZATION. *Urbanization* es la traducción que conviene a la primera acepción anotada a la izquierda, de preeminencia del medio urbano. Se usa mucho *development* para las residencias secundarias o barrios de casas de descanso o veraneo.

URBANO. *Urbano* has the same uses as *urban*.

URBAN, URBANE. *Urban* es *urbano*, relativo a la ciudad. (**Most megacities lack urban planning.** La mayoría de las megaciudades carecen de planificación urbana.) *Urbane* quiere decir *cortés*, *educado*. (**John is an urbane young man.** Juan es un joven bien educado.)

UTILIDAD. *Utilidad* is *benefit*, *profit*. (**Las utilidades de este año superaron a las del anterior.** This year's profit was greater than last year's.) It also means *usefulness*. (**Es un artilugio de utilidad dudosa.** It is a gadget of doubtful usefulness.)

UTILITY. *Utility* quiere decir (*empresa de*) *servicios públicos*. (**Electricity and gas have become indispensable utilities.** La electricidad y el gas se han vuelto servicios públicos indispensables.) En informática, se designa con la misma palabra a programas de uso generalizado. (**Anti-virus and other utilities are offered with your purchase.** Con su compra se brindan programas antivirus y otros.)

VAGO. *Vago* has the English equivalents *tramp, vagrant,* and *loafer.* (**Había vagos recorriendo la playa.** You could see vagrants walking on the beach.) *Terreno vago* is an *unimproved plot of land.*

VAGÓN. A *vagón* is a carriage that forms part of a train. (**El tren esta ba compuesto de vagones de primera y segunda clase.** The train had first- and second-class compartments.)

VALOR. The Spanish *valor* has meanings common to the English *value: cost, evaluation, principles, stock,* etc.

VARIACIÓN. *Variation* and *variación* share the same meaning. (**La variación matemática era descartable.** The mathematical variation was negligible.)

VAGUE. *Vague* quiere decir *indefinido, incierto, impreciso.* (**A vague rumor caused serious concern.** Un rumor impreciso provocó una grave inquietud.)

WAGON. *Wagon* es un vehículo diferente del vagón. Puede aplicarse a un *carromato, furgón* o hasta *cochecito* de juguete. (**The Amish traveled in oxen- or horse-drawn wagons.** Los Amish viajaban en carromatos tirados por bueyes o caballos.)

VALOR, VALUE. *Valor* es *coraje, valentía.* (**The hero was given the Medal of Valor.** El héroe recibió la Medalla al Valor.) En transacciones bancarias se suele poner *Value 8/7/2005*, por ejemplo, lo que quiere decir que el crédito o débito se hará efectivo en esa fecha.

VARIATION, VARIANCE (AT). Si alguien o algo está *at variance with*, significa que *se desvía, discrepa* o *está en desacuerdo.* (**The government practice is at variance with their declared principles.** La acción del gobierno difiere de los principios que proclama.)

VENTURA, AVENTURA. *Aventura* is the exact equivalent of *adventure*. *Ventura* is *fortune, chance*. *La buenaventura* means the *future read by a fortune-teller*. (**Una quiromántica le leyó la buenaventura.** She had her future told by a palm reader.)

VENTURE, ADVENTURE. *Aventura* es *adventure*. *Venture* significa *empresa comercial*, con una cierta connotación de incertidumbre o novedad. (**Some entrepreneurs and the government formed a joint venture to develop new products.** Algunos empresarios y el gobierno formaron una empresa mancomunada para fabricar productos nuevos.)

VERNÁCULO. *Vernáculo* means *national, indigenous*. (**Cultiva el folklore vernáculo.** He interprets the local folklore.)

VERNACULAR. *The vernacular* es la *jerga* o el *dialecto* local. (**In New York, the vernacular includes Italian and Yiddish words.** En Nueva York la jerga local incluye voces italianas e idish.)

VERSÁTIL. *Versátil* has negative connotations: *unstable, changing, unreliable*. (**Es muy versátil, cambia de un día para otro.** He is unstable; he changes from one day to the next.)

VERSATILE. La voz inglesa de este par significa *flexible, polifacetico, dúctil*. (**Being versatile, he can be assigned many different tasks.** Por ser flexible, se le pueden encomendar muchas tareas diferentes.)

VETERANO. Both words share the notion of *former, experienced, senior*. (**Después de una carrera como gran tenista, mi amigo juega en la categoría de veteranos.** After a career as a great tennis player, my friend competes in the senior category.)

VETERAN. La acepción anotada se complementa con la de *ex combatiente*, sobre todo en Estados Unidos. (**Care in veteran hospitals is one of the many privileges given to former soldiers.** Uno de los muchos privilegios de ex combatientes es la atención en hospitales reservados.)

VIAJE. *Viaje* is a specific *trip.* *Viajar* is *travel* in general. (**Están de viaje.** They are traveling.)

VOYAGE. *Voyage* indica específicamente una *travesía, un viaje por aire o por mar*, mientras que *travel* es un término genérico. (**Their long voyage will take them to three continents.** En su larga travesía recorrerán tres continentes.) En inglés suele utilizarse la expresión ***Bon voyage!*** para una despedida.

VICARIO. See column at right.

VICARIOUS. Partiendo del significado original de *vicario* como una autoridad eclesiástica superior, delegada del Señor, se da en utilizar el adjetivo *vicarious* por *delegado, indirecto.* (**I feel a vicarious pride at the success of my friends.** Me enorgullecen indirectamente los éxitos de mis amigos.)

VICIOSO. Maybe the most common use of *vicioso* is not *depraved* but *addicted.* (**Es un fumador vicioso.** He is an addicted smoker.)

VICIOUS. *Vicious* es *perverso, malsano, depravado, rencoroso.* (**His reaction was as vicious as could be expected from a wicked individual.** Su reacción fue tan perversa como cabía esperar de un individuo malvado.)

Vigilante. *Vigilante* is the popular name for *policeman* in some Latin American countries. (**Los vigilantes son muy mal remunerados.** Policemen have low pay.)

Vigilant, Vigilante. De la acepción general—*el que vigila*, o *vigilant*—se ha pasado a usar la palabra española *vigilante* para designar a los guardias urbanos auto-designados. (**The recent burglaries kept him vigilant.** Los robos recientes lo mantienen vigilante. **The vigilantes took justice into their own hands.** Los guardias particulares se tomaron la justicia en sus manos.)

Villa. *Villa* denotes both the *luxury residence* reminiscent of Roman villas, and a *village*. (**Tradicionalmente, se habla de la villa y corte de Madrid.** "The village and court of Madrid" is a traditional expression.)

Villa. En inglés, esta palabra se emplea normalmente para describir una residencia lujosa en el campo, pero que también puede ser urbana. (**The villa was guarded by armed men.** Guardaba la villa gente armada.)

Virtual. *Virtual* very often means *computerized*. (**Un método virtual.** A procedure by computer.) There are more and more *telefonistas virtuales* who answer standard queries.

Virtual. *Virtual* quiere decir *posible*, así como *implícito*, *tácito*, y se emplea cada vez más para designar a un método cibernético de hacer algo. (**With his impressive background, he is the virtual winner of the election.** Con sus notables antecedentes, es el ganador implícito de las elecciones.)

Vivo y en directo (En). A tautology used to describe a TV show broadcast live, directly from where it is produced.

VOLUBLE. This word means *fickle, changeable, inconstant.* (**"La donna è mobile" puede traducirse como la mujer es voluble.** The aria may be translated as "Woman is fickle.")

VOLUBLE. En inglés, *voluble* significa *verboso*. (**He is annoyingly voluble.** Es molesto con su cháchara.) Además, significa *giratorio, rotativo*.

VULGAR. In Spanish, *vulgar* has different meanings, not only *coarse, unrefined,* but also *common, popular*. (**Tiene una lengua vulgar.** He speaks very coarsely. **Es un producto vulgar.** It is a product commonly found.)

VULGAR. En inglés también se encuentra la acepción de *popular* para **vulgar**. (**Romance languages originated in vulgar Latin.** Las lenguas romances derivan del latín popular.)

YANQUI. In most Latin American countries, a US citizen is known as a *yanqui* (*yankee*), in others as *gringos*, the latter also applied to foreigners in general. (**Hay muchos yanquis en Francia.** There are many Americans in France.)

YANKEE. *Yankee* designa al habitante de un estado del noreste de los Estados Unidos. Durante la guerra civil, se oponía a los confederados, de los estados del sur. (**The yankees fought the confederates.** Los yanquis combatieron a los confederados.)

ZERO IN. Quiere decir *centrar la puntería* sobre un blanco, *aproximarse al objetivo*. (**The essay zeroed in on the objections to the policy.** El artículo fue concentrándose en las objeciones a la política.)

Bibliography – *Bibliografía*

Allen, Robert (consulting ed.). *The Penguin Dictionary*. London: Penguin Reference, 2004.

Gómez, Tana de (ed.). Diccionario Internacional. *English-Spanish Spanish-English*. New York: Simon & Schuster, undated.

Gómez de Silva, Guido. *Breve diccionario etimológico de la lengua española*. México: Fondo de Cultura Económica, 1988.

Prado, Marcial. *NTC's Dictionary of Spanish False Cognates*. Chicago: NTC Publishing Group, undated.

Real Academia Española. Diccionario de la lengua española. Vigésima quinta edición. Edición en CD-rom. Versión 1.0. Madrid: (DRAE), 2004.

Seco, Manuel, Olimpia Andrés, Gabino Ramos. *Diccionario abreviado del español actual*. Madrid: Aguilar Lexicografía, 2000.

Sierra Nava, Ramón. *Repertorio breve de disparates*. Madrid: Edición del autor, 2003.

Torrents dels Prats, Alfonso. *Diccionario de dificultades del inglés*. Barcelona: Diccionarios Juventud, 1976.

Spanish Word Index

English Word Index

About the Author

RAÚL GÁLER (Córdoba, Argentina, 1929) studied Economics at the University of Buenos Aires, but his main interest was languages. Starting in 1949, he had a long career at the United Nations, where he worked as shorthand reporter, editor and Spanish interpreter in New York and Geneva. In Geneva, he held the position of Chief of the Interpretation Service.

Printed in the United States
205248BV00005B/1-135/P